...And Thy Neighbor

...And Thy Neighbor

SAM SHOEMAKER
Talk About Creative Living . . .

Arranged By
Cecile Cox Offill

FOREWORD BY
The Right Reverend Bishop Cuthbert Bardsley, Lord
Bishop of Coventry Cathedral, Coventry, England

WORD BOOKS WACO, TEXAS

First Printing December, 1967
Second Printing March, 1968

Library of Congress Catalog Card Number: 67-26935

Printed in the United States of America

THIS BOOK IS LOVINGLY DEDICATED TO
ELLEN WHITRIDGE SHOEMAKER JOHNSTON
BELOVED SISTER OF SAMUEL MOOR SHOEMAKER

FOREWORD

DOCTOR SAMUEL SHOEMAKER was a great prophet, a great lover, a great man of God.

He was a great prophet, and there are not many in any one generation. I first heard Doctor Shoemaker speak in the year 1929. It was an inspiring but terrifying experience. It had upon me the impact which all true prophecy should have; it made me glad and sad. It made me cry out "Thanks be to God," and it made me exclaim "Woe is me."

Doctor Shoemaker spoke like a machine gun! The words poured forth in a torrent. He gave one the feeling that he had much to say and very little time in which to say it. He was ablaze with a passionate conviction, filled with a deep concern—unlike some preachers he was convinced about the reality and the love of God and overflowing with a deep concern—unlike some preachers he was convinced about the crack of a rifle. At that time I was a young theological student, immature, uncertain of myself, of my vocation and of the future. Dr. Shoemaker filled me with a great hope—he made me believe that life under God's control was a thrilling adventure and that Jesus Christ was a completely reliable Saviour who would never let one down, never let one off but never let one go. Since that moment, over 30 years ago, I have heard him preach on many occasions. Always, and increasingly, I have realized that I was in the presence of one of the great prophetic voices of the world.

He was also a great lover. He seemed to wrap his arms

around mankind. He made each person feel that he was the one person in the world who really mattered. For, in addition to being a quite outstanding preacher, he was one of the few really great evangelists. Men and women by the thousands came into his study defeated, hopeless and helpless. They left an hour later, having made their peace with God. He brought us face to face with ourselves and with Jesus Christ. Sam Shoemaker was no sentimentalist. He loved the sinner, but he hated sin.

And he would wrestle and work and plead and pray until the sinner had gone beneath layer after layer of unreality and make-believe to the real person. Then, and only then, did he introduce us to the real Saviour.

At the back of all this prophecy and evangelism lay his holiness. He was a man of God who said his prayers. Indeed, his life was a prayer. This is not to say that he was dour or off-putting—far from it—he was one of the most humorous men I have ever met, with a fund of amusing stories second to none. But underneath all his gay humor and true worldliness lay this unmistakable holiness. He was a man of God, who knew God and who lived in the Presence of God.

Such men are rare. In any one generation there are only a few men of the stature of Doctor Shoemaker. Just because of this, one must be grateful to Mrs. Offill for bringing together these sermons so that "he who is dead may yet speak." I hope that this book will have a world-wide circulation and that many may find through this book an experience of the saving and transforming love of Jesus Christ. Such miracles of rebirth will be the best memorial to a great prophet, a great lover and a great man of God.

CUTHBERT BARDSLEY
COVENTRY

PREFACE

This book is a sampling of the sermons preached toward the end of his ministry by the late Rev. Canon Samuel Shoemaker, and circulated by the vestry of Calvary Episcopal Church of Pittsburgh, Pennsylvania, under the title of "This Week's Word."

What these sermons meant in the lives of the people who received them can best be told by the people themselves. Testimony of the power of "This Week's Word" to touch and change lives came to "Dr. Sam" in hundreds of grateful letters from all over the world. A few of these letters (alas, there is room for so few) have been chosen for use with each sermon as witness to Canon Shoemaker's far-reaching ministry both at the time the sermons were given and as, through the mails, they brought faith and hope to countless numbers of people.

It was because of those letters that this book was undertaken. On a raw day in March, shortly after Dr. Sam retired from his parish in Pittsburgh, I met his secretary who had been in charge of the mailing and correspondence for "This Week's Word."

"Would you like to see some of the letters which came to Dr. Sam about 'This Week's Word'?" she asked. "I have cartons of them and it seems a shame not to share them before I throw them away."

Thus, the cartons of letters were transferred from my

church to my home. As I read, I was amazed and moved both by the number and diversity of the man and women, young and old, from every walk of life, in almost every country of the world who expressed their appreciation of "This Week's Word."

In imagination I could see the Baltimore doctor who had written to Dr. Sam to say that he considered "This Week's Word" the most important periodical that came into his home, and later as he described in a letter to me his afternoon with Dr. Sam in the the garden at Burnside, the home of the Shoemaker family. That Methodist minister in a lonely South African village came alive as I read his letter to this man in the United States to whom he wrote, "Your words are more help to me as I minister to this troubled land than any other words I read except the words of the Bible." And the druggist in the small Virginia town was very real as he told Dr. Sam of the manager of the Hilton Hotel in Chicago who had had struck off 5000 copies of a sermon called "What the Church can learn from Alcoholics Anonymous" which were placed on the newsstand of the hotel for free distribution.

Although I had heard these same sermons from my own church pew, it was not until I read these letters that I realized the power of even the printed words and the radio voice of our rector, Canon Shoemaker, as his vast audience was enlarged week after week. The conviction grew that at least a few of these sermons should be published in book form to project this faith and hope to those who now could not, otherwise, feel the contagion of Dr. Sam's joy in Christ, his clarity of mind, and above all, his love and concern for all mankind.

When I wrote to Canon Shoemaker of such a book he was dubious. Finally, he wrote, "Well, if you feel as strongly as you do about these sermons you may be guided. If so I will help you all I can." About publication of a few of the letters he wrote characteristically (for he was a man of real and rare humility), "If the letters are in praise of God and what He means to men I am for them as I believe in the value of witness for Christ. If they are in praise of Sam Shoemaker, however, they are not relevant." It is as a witness then, both to God and to the effectiveness of His channel, Sam Shoemaker, that the letters are included with the sermons.

One day during the summer of the year after Dr. Sam retired, he and I were in his study trying to choose from the hundreds of sermons the ones to be used for the book.

"There are three urgencies that follow me wherever I am," said Dr. Sam.

"One is how to help people in trouble; another is how to help them to know that Jesus Christ is the answer; and the third is how to help them to learn what the Holy Spirit can do if only they will let Him come into their lives."

After a long pause, Canon Shoemaker picked up a used envelope from his desk and scribbled on it and gave it to me. On it he had written, "Part One, *Are you in Trouble?*' Part Two, *Jesus Christ is the Answer.*' Part Three, *What the Holy Spirit Can Do.*' Choose the sermons to fit into these categories," he said. This we have done.

The real author of the book, of course, is Dr. Sam himself. But it has many other authors who belong to the far-flung scattered brotherhood of his devoted and grateful friends who gladly have given permission that their letters be used.

In his book, *A Young Man's View of the Ministry,* Dr. Shoemaker said, "Most of us will not be very long remembered after we are gone, and I, for one, prefer to make the investment of my life in the things that will not perish, in the immortal stuff of human character."

Both sermons and letters in our book are a living testimony of Sam Shoemaker's investment of his life in the "immortal stuff of human character." We offer the book as a dedication and a trust, and with the prayer that "he who is dead may yet speak."

May Dr. Sam's words, his work and his life long continue to pay dividends in the building of the Kingdom of God.

C.C.O.

ACKNOWLEDGEMENTS

I should like to make grateful acknowledgement to the vestry of Calvary Episcopal Church of Pittsburgh, Pennsylvania, for their wisdom and generosity in the printing and circulation of these sermons which were preached by their rector, the late Rev. Samuel Moor Shoemaker, during the last years of his ministry; and to Mrs. Helen Smith Shoemaker for permission to publish her late husband's sermons. Our grateful thanks go also to the present rector and staff of Calvary Episcopal Church of Pittsburgh, for their encouragement and help in bringing this book to print.

It is with deep personal gratitude that we thank Miss Helen Clay Frick, Canon Shoemaker's devoted friend, for belief in, and encouragement of the project since its inception; we are grateful to Miss Grace Lumpkin and Miss Louise Townsend Nicholl for their unflagging encouragement and editorial help.

We feel we express the appreciation of Dr. Sam, as well as our own, for the sensitive Foreword written by the Right Reverend Bishop Cuthbert Bardsley, the Lord Bishop of Coventry Cathedral of Coventry, England, and a lifelong friend of Dr. Sam.

Our thanks go also to Canon Shoemaker's many friends, old and new, who have given permission that their letters to and from him to be published. We wish to thank also the many friends and admirers of Canon Shoemaker, who have given long hours to typing and proofreading of this work, and have made the task a pleasant one; as have the responses from staff members of the many Christian movements in which "Dr. Sam" occupies a permanently organic place, i.e. The Pittsburgh Experiment, Faith At Work, Young Life, World Neighbors, etc.

Grateful acknowledgement is made to the following for permission to use copyright material:

E. P. DUTTON AND CO., INC., PUBLISHERS
A quotation from *How You Can Help Other People* by Canon Samuel Shoemaker, copyright 1946.

THE LIVING CHURCH FOUNDATION, INC.
A quotation from *The Living Church*, November 22, 1959.

LIFE SYNDICATION
A quotation from "Too Late The Phalarope" by Alan Paton, *Life*, December 22, 1955.

THE DIVISION OF CHRISTIAN EDUCATION OF THE NATIONAL COUNCIL OF THE CHURCHES OF CHRIST
Quotations from The Revised Standard Version of the Bible, copyright, 1946 and 1952.

DODD, MEAD AND COMPANY
A quotation from *Orthodoxy* by G. K. Chesterton.

YALE UNIVERSITY PRESS
A quotation from *The Courage To Be* by Paul Tillich.

RANDOM HOUSE
A quotation from *Witness* by Whittaker Chambers.

CHARLES SCRIBNER'S SONS
A quotation from *Spirit, Son and Father* by Henry P. Van Dusen.

THE MACMILLAN COMPANY
A quotation from *The Case For Christianity* by C. S. Lewis. Copyright 1943, 1945, 1952 by The Macmillan Company. Used by permission.

HENRY REGNERY COMPANY PUBLISHERS
A quotation from *The Conservative Mind* by Kirk Russell. Copyright 1953, 1954.

HARPER AND ROW PUBLISHERS, INC.
A quotation from *Report To The Creator* by Jerome Ellison. Copyright 1956.
Quotations from *By The Power Of God, The Experiment Of Faith,* and *With The Holy Spirit And With Power,* by Samuel M. Shoemaker.
A quotation from *History Of The Expansion Of Christianity* by Kenneth Latourette.

Note: Every effort has been made to locate copyright holders of all quoted material for the purpose of obtaining permission for use and for giving proper credit. Indulgence is begged in the event of any unintentional omissions.

CONTENTS

Part Three

WHAT THE HOLY SPIRIT CAN DO

PART ONE

ARE *YOU* YOURSELF IN TROUBLE?
OR YOUR NEIGHBOR, YOUR CHURCH,
YOUR COUNTRY, YOUR WORLD?

CHAPTER 1

WHAT DO YOU DO
WHEN THE RAFT COMES APART?

"We wonder what a God of love has to do with evil, but we do know that he has to do with how we meet evil, whether with faith and victory, or with self-pity and defeat."

From
"Dealing with the Darkness of God"
By
Samuel Moor Shoemaker

Sometime ago I was visiting at a school which is situated on a high bluff above a river. As we looked down into it, one of the masters told me about a boy who tied together a couple of pieces of wood for a raft, and launched himself in the swift-moving waters of the river. Out in the rapids the ropes gave way and the raft came apart. They saw him and got him in time to get him out safely when he was in real danger of being swept under. This master said to me, "Preach a sermon some time on what you do when the raft comes apart."

Now I would guess that the first thing that lad tried to

1

do was to tie the pieces together. Failing that, if he could not keep his balance in the water (and it was very cold), I suppose he looked for a limb that might hang out over the current which he might be able to touch. I suppose he called for help. Until the help arrived, my guess would be that he did a very quick review of his life and probably did a little praying; for there are times when our situation puts us beyond the help of other people and we cannot help ourselves. Finally he was helped out of the current by others.

Personal and Public Danger

Not very many of us have experienced just what he experienced. But for most of us, at one time or another, the raft has come apart. We found ourselves suddenly without our expected income. Someone we trusted implicitly played us false. One day our health was apparently perfect, and the next day we had a heart attack. We looked forward to leisure after retirement, and we found the time on our hands unbearable. We formed a partnership that had in it all kinds of promise, and distrust grew up between the other partner and ourselves till we had to give it up. One could name a thousand things that can happen in life as full of apparent disaster as what confronted the boy on the raft.

Unfortunately in our time, it is not alone our little personal rafts that have come apart: it is the rafts of the world on which we thought we were sailing or drifting towards greater peace and security. Science has become the god of many in our time; but science may have brought us to the edge of an abyss. We have expected our representatives in Washington, and our international statesmen at the United Nations to provide peace and safety for us, without remembering that these men cannot go very far beyond the levels on which people at home are willing to live; and we know we scarcely deserve the peace we long for. Never has the world seen a force so ready to break the slender strands that hold together the web of civilization as are the Communists: they have set fuses under every pile of tinder in the world that they can touch, and no man knows when it might all go up in smoke. Two of the wise spiritual guides of our time have spoken to this point. Thomas R. Kelly, in *Testament of Devotion* said, "An awful solemnity is upon the earth, for the last vestige of earthly security is gone. . . . The plagues of Egypt are upon the world . . . and there is no escape for you or for me." And Dr. Elton Trueblood says, "Millions are fatalistic. They feel utterly powerless in the presence of forces they can neither understand nor control."

What do we do when the personal raft, or the world raft, comes apart?

Life IS Dangerous

If we have time and capacity to think, we do well to remember that for many lives and for most ages the periods without trouble are few and far between. It is only a very feckless person who thinks he or she will come through the whole of life without serious difficulty. It is only a very egoistic age that thinks the major ills of humanity have been resolved. With all progress there seems to come also a progression in problems to be solved. Let us never think that fate—still less that God—has singled out either ourselves or our generation for special misfortune or anguish. Only the most self-centered and petty people think in this way. There is something honorable, or at least characteristically human, in undergoing trouble. And if you want to get yourself wound in a real difficulty, try to imagine a world made already perfect, with no possibility of evil or suffering and try to wring any vestige of meaning or significance out of such an automatically good world. It looks as if trouble must have some place in the divine and human scheme.

What Happens and How We Take What Happens

The next thought that may help us is the realization that in human life there are always two things: there is what happens, and there is how we take what happens. We cannot often control what happens.

The polio falls upon the well-loved child; or the fatal shot is fired in some distant place that sets war in motion. But we can nearly always control how we take what happens. I know a family where polio struck; it brought them all into a profoundly deeper spiritual relation. The boy who had it has come through a long, painful but almost complete recovery, and is going into the ministry.

It is hard to find much good in war; but we have seen people react even to war with courage and unselfishness, and millions upon millions of them have made the best of it that they could. This fact that while we cannot control what happens, we can control how we take what happens, is the sure sign to us that character is superior to circumstances, and faith is greater than fate. Most trouble proves in the end to be a kind of test. Meeting a failure with courage and good spirit is a kind of success; and many an evil when overcome seems justified. A man in my work is much more borne up than borne down by the human trouble with which he comes in contact . . . for he sees a great deal of quiet human courage, faith and serenity of spirit. Our best occupation in this world is not to try to avoid trouble, but to see if we can meet it as it should be met, not only with courage that is not broken by it, but with faith that saves us from defeat. The Christian religion is no guarantee against trouble; it is a guarantee against defeat.

Just how does our faith help us when the raft comes apart?

God Is With Us In Our Difficulty

Let us remember that God did not create the world and then give it a push and withdraw. God has always loved the world; and therefore He gave His only-begotten Son that in Him we might find redemption. Christ did not take His stand on some distant star and call down His messages to us because the world was too evil for Him to participate in its life at all; He came into the world as Man. He was poor, lived in a small country, was persecuted and executed. We might say the raft began coming apart for Him when He saw the inevitability of the Cross. He kept walking straight toward it because He knew His mission of salvation for mankind could only be accomplished by His own sacrifice. Let us remember that thus God shared our human limitations and sufferings. Christ understands our disappointments, losses, tragedies: He knew them personally. "In the world ye shall have tribulation," He said—that was His realistic evaluation of life. "But be of good cheer, I have overcome the world"—that was His promise of faith and of victory through faith (John 16:33).

Place Your Own Faults

Then let us try to face honestly where our own mistakes or failures may have brought about this trouble. A lot of us ask God to get us out of our predicaments which our sins have gotten us into, when we ought to ask Him to help us get rid of our sins instead. I do not believe God punishes people to get even or square up the account with us, but I certainly believe God teaches us through our tribulations if we are willing to learn. We do not break moral laws; we go up against them and they break us. That is true of physical laws, and it is true of moral and spiritual ones also. Let us try to be very honest with God, with ourselves, and perhaps with some trusted human adviser who will not just sympathize with us and let us down, but will help us to deal realistically with ourselves. It was foolish for that lad to get out on that raft in the first place; and this must have impressed itself on him when he had time to think how close a brush with disaster he had. There are traits in us, impulses, carelessnesses, which may be closely connected with our misfortunes. The great problem is always the willingness to see ourselves as we are, and to want to be different. Only God, I think, can give us the grace for this. Like a good father, He helps us see our mistakes, all the while holding out to us forgiveness and strength and new life if we will take them.

Surrender the Situation and Ourselves

We must also seek to surrender this situation to Him. Here is a great loss, disillusionment, anguish of mind or body. Humanly we can only meet it with a stoic courage, or with dumb resignation, or with frantic rebellion. If we will take our hands off it, however, and stop trying to handle it in our own way, inviting God in on it and honestly asking Him what He wants us to to do in the situation, we may be surprised at what happens. Let us seek to quiet our emotions about it all, and to pray—not so much asking that this or that should come about, as that we be guided by God as to how He wants us to meet the situation and handle it. Only so can God come into the situation, when we are willing to put aside our wilfulness and pride and hurt feelings, and let Him control what we do. We need to do this in connection with the world situation, as well as with our private troubles, asking that His will be sought by all and prevail. Wilfulness and fear and personal emotion subside when we really pray. Prayer is intended not to change God's mind, but to find it.

The Problem of Pride

Now before all this can happen, before we can meet situations in any such spirit as this, something needs to happen to us. In the end, somebody had to come and get that lad on the raft, and save him, for he was beyond the place where he could save himself. In these days of man's magnificent accomplishments in scientific fields, and as a result of our largely secularistic education, many people have come to feel that human wisdom can manage just about everything. This is of the essence of pride, for it really puts man in the place of God. Is there no connection between our human pride and our human predicament at this time? I think there is! We never knew so much as we do today, we never could do so much, we never travelled so fast or knew the news so quickly. Yet we never were nearer to the brink of total disaster. We need to be saved from our pride before it destroys us. We do not need mere ethical guidance from God, we need to be saved from our sins and from their consequences if God be so merciful to us. Most of us want exemption from the consequences but freedom to keep on with the sins. It can't be done. Men and nations alike must come back to God, and ask God for forgiveness and for redemption. This is the beginning of wisdom.

Let me tell you how this has worked out in two concrete situations where the "raft came apart."

I know a woman who for nearly six years has been suffering from the effects of a terrible motor accident. The hospitalization has eaten up nearly all the family savings, beside pain and wonder whether she would ever walk again. So great has been her faith and quiet courage that literally dozens of people's lives have been changed by the way she met this tragic loss of mobility and health. She is walking again; but from the first moment it happened faith went to work. God worked through her faith, and the net result has been a glorious victory over a tragic circumstance. God can wholly change what we make of a tragedy if we surrender the situation and ourselves to Him.

A family had three wonderful children. A little understood disease attacked them one after another, and all three have died. I have not seen a greater family tragedy in my experience. These people have a quiet, sturdy faith. I do not think they understand why this happened, any more than the rest of us do. It was a hard assignment that life offered them. They met it, not with rebellion nor resignation, but with a selfless kind of courage that has inspired their friends. They have taken up their lives and are living for other people because of the unselfish courage which their faith in God has given them.

Everything depends upon the kind of faith we bring to life. The point is never whether life has put upon us too much of a burden, or too heavy a trial, but whether we meet this with faith and courage, or with fear and self-centeredness. I have been told that on the evening when it looked as if Britain might be invaded, and things looked darkest during the last war, Sir Winston called his cabinet together and told them the worst. He withheld no facts. They listened gravely. Then he leaned back in his chair and said, "And you know, I find it all rather inspiring!" That is the kind of faith we need.

So, whether we face personal tribulation, or the larger perils of our inflammable world, God is there to help. Perhaps the greatest word of faith about God's power to transform all life is in St. Paul's magnificent declaration in Romans 8, "All things work together for good to them that love God." That is the victory of faith that overcomes the world!

"Comfort comes from faith in God. It is not a comfort that exempts us from trouble. It comes to us right in the midst of trouble, pain, anxiety, disappointment, loss."

From
The Comfort of God
By
Samuel Moor Shoemaker

(From letter to S.M.S. from M.W.)

Dixon, Illinois
September 31, 1961

Dear Dr. S:

I have just received your sermon, "What Do You Do When The Raft Comes Apart?", and it has given me courage to go on. For ten months my mother has been dying and I have given up teaching to care for her. It is what I want to do, but how not to fail her and to see it through!

Then comes your sermon which makes me know that I *can* see it through, with God's help, even though I am so tired.

Thank you for this sermon when I needed it most.

Gratefully,
M. W.

(From letter written by M.W. to C.C.O., after Dr. Shoemaker died.)

Dixon, Illinois
March 1963

Dear Mrs. O:

Thank you for writing me of Dr. Shoemaker's death. He will live with me always.

I remember so well what he wrote to me after my mother died, and I had told him about it. 'Like a bird, we can rise on the very wind that blows against us if our wings are stretched out into space,' he wrote.

I still read the sermons from "This Week's Word" as I have kept every one of them, and the one about which I first wrote him was "What Do You Do When The Raft Comes Apart". It was a part of my life during my mother's long illness.

The one called, "Don't Pigeonhole People", I try to read before I begin my teaching each day. I teach music to eighty children and young people, and this sermon helps me not to form pre-conceptions of these children because of their backgrounds, etc.

I am still learning from "Dr. Sam" to try to understand the emotional needs of the people I may influence.

I come back to "This Week's Word" when I want inspirational reading which has a challenge that changes my own attitudes and actions, too.

I have read much such since "This Week's Word" stopped coming, but I have found nothing else as helpful.

May you be blessed in your work to keep him alive to help others.

Sincerely,
M. W.

CHAPTER 2

. . . AND THY NEIGHBOR
AS THYSELF

LUKE 10:27

"When Christ commanded us to love our neighbors as ourselves He was commanding us to love ourselves. If we will let ourselves be drawn back into God's love, we will find that we cannot go on hating that which God loves."

From
Commandment 2B—As Thyself
By
Samuel Moor Shoemaker

Most of us are familiar with what is called the "Summary of the Law." A lawyer tried to put Jesus to the test, seeking I suspect to find out whether He was "orthodox" or not. He asked, "What shall I do that I may inherit eternal life?" And Jesus referred him right back to the Law which he accepted, and asked him what he read there. It was the lawyer, not Jesus, who gave this summary, "Thou shalt love the Lord thy God with all thy heart and with all thy soul, and with all thy mind; and thy neighbor as thyself." Jesus commended him for this, and told him if he really did it, he would "live."

Two Kinds of Love

Here are two kinds of love—the love of God, and the love of other human beings. Different as they are, they are cognate and inseparable. They occur together in this passage, but the love of God comes first. I believe we are meant to think about them as two parts of the same thing.

Of course, it is hard to know what a person means when he uses the word "love". Dr. Alec Vidler complains that "it covers all types of affection that range from Hollywood to heaven." But most of us know that its connotations are various, and we know which ones apply in this Christian connection though we might have difficulty in defining them. We know when we are practising love and when we are falling down on it. We know still better when other people are practising it towards us, and when they are falling down on it!

Loving Ourselves

"Thy neighbor as thyself." It appears as if the primary and given factor here is our love of ourselves. "As thyself." Nowhere are we more likely to make a complete gap between what we say, and what we really feel and intend to do, than here. We say, "It's a sin to love yourself, and a Christian can't do it, so I never do." But actually most of us take care of ourselves first and best, and others get what is left over. Some of this is inevitable, and some of it is right. We must try to find out something of what our Lord meant when He accepted this word from the lawyer.

The Eternal Triangle

We are beginning to learn from psychologists what religion has been telling us all along, that we are only "persons" as we are in relation to other persons. And the greatest other

Person is God. So that we are bound into a triangle, of God, other people, and ourselves—or (to be more realistic) ourselves, other people, and God. We easily see that we must have a relation to other people or to God: we do not so easily see that we also need a "relation" to ourselves. Jesus indicated that there should be such a relation when He accepted the phrase "thy neighbor as thyself;" if we can love ourselves, there must be a relation between different sides of ourselves. And the simple psychological fact is that, unless we are in good relation with ourselves, we shall not be in good relation with others, and we shall not even be in good relation with God. Oftentimes we do not understand others because we do not understand ourselves, and we do not understand ourselves because we do not understand others, and we do not understand either because we do not understand God and the way He works with people and in life.

Self-Acceptance

What should be our relation to ourselves? How can we, as Christians, love ourselves in such a way as to enhance our love for other people and for God? We surely are not to be uncritically pleased with ourselves. We surely are not to be so critical of ourselves that we feel ourselves always wrong. We must, it comes to me, accept ourselves, as we are, long enough to get some leverage upon ourselves. We must also accept some clear goal and ideal for ourselves which does not fluctuate. We must accept our necessity to travel towards that goal without too much delay, and yet without the prodding of an impossibly "perfectionist" hurry. There are imperfections, they will not be eradicated quickly, but they need to be eradicated and as fast as can be done with moral sincerity. With this understanding, we can accept ourselves, and even enjoy ourselves a good deal of the time. Dr. Nels Ferre says, "Acceptance and enjoyment of self are not to be confused with self-love" and then he tells why: "For self-acceptance is self-forgetful within community, whereas a self-love always has invidious other-reference." I think this means that outgoingness towards others is blocked by real self-love, but helped by genuine self-acceptance. I believe self-acceptance to mean that I shall always be a partial and imperfect person, failing and sinning sometimes, but also with capacity to do better with the help of God. There is an inevitable tension here between encouragement and discouragement concerning myself, both of which need to be accepted without lingering too long over them: we must get on with the real business of living!

It is this kind of understanding, I think, that underlies Jesus' accepting the lawyer's summary, including loving the neighbor "as thyself." Only such a person can love, in any constructive fashion. Dr. David E. Roberts said that "even the clearest, most cogent ethical principle can be empty and tyrannical unless it is accompanied by whole-heartedness ('feeling for self') and sympathy ('feeling for others')." Obviously "whole-heartedness" can only come from a person reasonably free within, and obviously "sympathy" can only come from such a person, for we must be to some real degree free from ourselves to love at all. But we are never free from ourselves until we accept ourselves in the way we are trying to describe. Dr. Roberts holds that "capacity to respond to God's love is directly related to self-love (self-acceptance)." Most of us realize, too, how important it is that we be loved and accepted by someone else before we can really believe that we are loved and accepted by God.

"Commandment 2B"

We have tried to deal with what a friend of mine calls "Commandment 2B," i.e., the love of self. This is the kind of person who is to love his neighbor; we must have a certain kind of self-knowledge and self-acceptance to do it at all. But if he has these things, wherein does this love for the neighbor consist?

It consists largely in realizing our neighbor's need to understand and accept himself in the same way. We are always so eager to see love in terms of "doing" something; and clearly enough there will be times when it is a mockery to talk about love and not "do" something. When a family needs food and we give it to them, helping a man find work when he does not have it, remembering the sick and poor and old, going the various kinds of "second mile" which are always so necessary in every kind of work on earth—these are essential. Some of our overflowing supplies in America should be going to people across the seas who do not have them, not for anything this will gain us, but just because they are in need. There will always be "works" of charity, but we must be sure there is charity behind the works. If what we give or do is grounded in a feeling of superiority, it is not love. If it is motivated by what it will "get" the giver, it is not love. If it is done to bring about an expression of thanks from the recipient (and often it is), it is not love. If it is done because it gives us a feeling of satisfaction and self-righteousness to do it, it is not love. The things we do must pour out from the thing we are, as water pours up out of a spring and a spring cannot help pouring out water. Mere warm amiability may not be love, but there will always be some warm amiability in love. "The gift without the giver is bare." We are meant to feel for the other person. If there is a hole in his shoe, our foot ought to be cold. And it may

well be that the spontaneity and feeling we have for him
is quite as important to him psychologically and spiritually
as anything material we can ever do.

From the Heart

Let us not, then, be superior to doing the simplest and
even most menial acts of service and kindness; they may be
indicated and in this world of human vicissitude and
tragedy they always will be. But let us beware lest what
we do be squeezed out of a narrow heart, or melted re-
luctantly from a cold one, or chipped with difficulty from
a hard one. There are many righteous and even generous,
but cold and hard people. They sometimes do what they
should, even to being generous; but they do not and cannot love, being themselves. They do not let themselves
feel, and so they cannot love. There is peculiar and special
danger of this in a day of so much public welfare, and of
so much giving through the impersonal checkbook. Medical
people are realizing that science, surgery and chemistry
are not enough. One of the problems in mental hospitals
is the problem of giving patients enough love to give them
hope. And we all know that there has grown up in ordinary
hospitals a new kind of therapy—it is in reality a very old
one. They call it "t.l.c."—tender loving care. For this there
is no substitute. Sick or well, people need it as they need
air and food and sleep.

The Christian religion ought to provide for us all an
inexhaustible supply of healthy, outgoing, transforming love
for other people. A church like this ought to be so filled with
it that when a stranger comes among us, he feels something
buoyant and pneumatic in the air. This does not mean that
you and I are better than other people, or more worthy to
bestow love on them: this means that you and I can be
and ought to be in touch with more love on which we can

draw and share with them. This must not be gushy and sentimental; far too many of us give others the sentimental caring we should like to receive from them. Neither do we have to be salesman personalities who have taken a Dale Carnegie course in getting along with people. I know some people who are even a little shy socially, who yet pour out a great deal of love to other people. If we are aiming to be real Christians, we shall be open to caring more for more people, and we shall be open to letting them care for us. There is nothing unselfish in what is sometimes called "keeping to myself," or even "keeping my troubles to myself." There is no value in running off at the mouth about our problems with everyone we meet, but all of us at times need to tell somebody what we are going through, and then be quiet enough to receive from them some understanding and maybe some word of counsel. Some are too dependent on others, but some are not dependent enough, and their independence constitutes a deep and dangerous pride. Love is always a two-way street. We both need it and need to give it.

Christian Fellowship

How many of us know what Christian fellowship is? Just sitting beside people or even working with them in church is not fellowship. Some people are lonely in church and would give anything to find Christian fellowship. If you really want it, the way to begin is to give it. Begin in friendliness and courtesy. This may start off rather experimentally. Speak to a stranger near you, and pray to be of mutual help. Love seeks to give not what we need, but what the other person needs. Love is not afraid to black someone's boots if need be: travelling with seven men, we missed one of them one afternoon before going out to a reception, and found him cleaning fourteen shoes! And love is not afraid to come into the deep places of human personality when this is indicated, where we talk about our lives, our problems, and the bearing of Christ upon them. A young man and new Christian in this parish was telling me the other evening of his first efforts to win another man who began by saying he was an atheist—and he made progress with him! We shall not press our faith upon others, especially our own brand of it; but the deepest human need is for God, and only believing people can meet that need. A phone call comes in at this point from another man in this parish, saying, "I'd like to talk to you for hours about the wonderful things God is doing!" Why do these things happen to and through him? Because he is one of the most deeply loving people I ever knew, and lives in the midstream of the Christian fellowship. Through people like this God can pour His love out into the world. The people who let themselves be loved by God are the people who can accept themselves, and then give themselves away in love to their neighbors.

And so does love become the channel by which God reaches out to others, even through us!

"Christianity is important here because it should give us no peace in the nurture of our prejudices. For a Christian there is but one kind of aristocracy, the aristocracy of the spirit."

From,
"The Holy Spirit and the Race Question"
By
Samuel Moor Shoemaker

(Quote from a letter to Canon Shoemaker from a prisoner in Virginia)

                                  May, 1960

Dear Dr. Shoemaker:

You will wonder what a poor Christian prisoner is doing writing to you.

I have been receiving your sermons from "This Week's Word," and they mean more to me than words can express. I have been in prison, convicted of murder, but I have become an ordained minister through a correspondence course in bible and theology. I teach bible courses on each Sunday morning, and I use your sermons.

Even though I am not living in society, you help me to know that I am a child of God because I have a feeling for all His people in this place.

Yours in Christ,
A.J.F., No. 375100

(From S.M.S. to A.J.F.)

Pittsburgh, Pa.
June, 1960

My dear Friend:

May God bless you and use you more and more to make known the great truths of Christ and His gospels to the men about you. Remember that St. Paul wrote some of his greatest letters from a prison cell.

Faithfully,
S. M. S.

(From letter to Canon Shoemaker from Mrs. I. W.)

Farmington, N. H.
June, 1961

Dear Dr. Shoemaker:

If you have any extra copies of ". . . *And Thy Neighbor As Thyself*," will you send them to me to take to some of my neighbors who are shut-ins?

I am a widow, and can't do much in money because I live on Social Security, but I have learned to try to do what you say in your sermons, trust God. For the 26 years since my husband died, God has provided for my needs. These sermons are my spiritual food, and I share them with as many of my neighbors as I can.

Thank you for "This Week's Word."

Sincerely,
(Mrs.) I. W.

(Letter to Canon Shoemaker from Miss R. L.)
South Carolina
April 16, 1961

Dear Dr. Shoemaker:

Thank you especially for the sermon called . . . *And Thy Neighbor* which came today. It seemed to speak directly to me.

For years I've been troubled about old, sick colored people in our county who have no one to care for them. I have talked to some of my own church people about this but have had feeble response.

What would you think of my writing to some of my rich friends asking them to help me establish a Rest Home for these old people? These are our neighbors surely, and this sermon has put them on my conscience.

With enthusiastic thanks for your ministry,

Gratefully,
R. C. L.

(From letter from Dr. Shoemaker to Miss L.)
Pittsburgh, Pa.
April 25, 1961

Dear Miss L.

. . . Pray for that Home for old people in your county. I just feel sure that God is going to put it into the heart of someone to make it possible since you have it so much on your heart. Stay with the idea, and pray for it, and I will too!

Faithfully,

S. M. S.

[After Canon Shoemaker died we wrote to ask Miss L. if her dream had materialized. Her answer was that only the Sunday before a large delegation of people of both races, many churches, fraternal organizations, etc. had attended the laying of cornerstone ceremonies for the D. County Rest Home. "By far the most help has come from the Negroes," she said. In 1964 she wrote of the dedication of the completed building by her own Episcopal bishop, and in 1967 she writes: "The Home is a going concern, although we have our troubles. But, by working together, we have achieved a measure of real integration 'of hearts' and my own church has stricken the 'Whites Only' clause from our by-laws by vote of the Vestry!

"Dr. Shoemaker did not know what he was starting when he circulated that sermon about neighbors!" C.O.]

CHAPTER 3

WHAT THE CHURCH
HAS TO LEARN
FROM ALCOHOLICS ANONYMOUS

"The commissioned custodian of the faith is the Church, and the Church has no other business than the teaching and application and spread of this faith."

From
"Down to Earth Religion"
By
Samuel Moor Shoemaker

". . . God chose what is foolish in the world to shame the wise, God chose what is weak in the world to shame the strong . . ."

I Corinthians 1:27, (RSV)

During the weekend of the Fourth of July last, I attended one of the most remarkable conventions I ever expect to attend. It was a gathering in St. Louis of about 5,000 members of the movement called Alcoholics Anonymous. The occasion was the celebration of their twentieth anniversary, and the turning over freely and voluntarily of the control and destiny of that great movement by the founders to a board which represents the fellowship as a whole.

23

As I lived and moved among these men and women for three days, I was moved as I have seldom been moved in my life. It happens that I have watched the unfolding of this movement with more than usual interest, for its real founder and guiding spirit, Bill W--------, found his initial spiritual answer at Calvary Church in New York when I was rector there in 1935. Having met two men, unmistakable alcoholics, who had found release from their difficulty, he was moved to seek out the same answer for himself. But he went further. Being of a foraging and inquiring mind, he began to think there was some general law operating here which could be made to work, not in two men's lives only, but in two thousand or two million. He set to work to find out what it was. He consulted psychiatrists, doctors, clergy and recovered alcoholics to discover what it was.

The first actual group was not in New York, but in Akron, Ohio. Bill was spending a weekend there in a hotel. The crowd was moving towards the bar. He was lonely and felt danger assailing him. He consulted the church directory in the hotel lobby, and found the name of a local clergyman and his church. He called him on the telephone and said, "I am an alcoholic down here at the hotel. The going is a little hard just now. Have you anybody you think I might meet and talk to?" He gave him the name of a woman who belonged to one of the great tire-manufacturing families. He called her, she invited him out at once and said she had a man she wanted to have meet him. While he was on his way, she called Dr. Bob S-------- and his wife, Anne. Dr. Bob said he'd give her five minutes. He stayed five hours and told Bill, "You're the only man I've ever seen with the answer to alcoholism." They invited Bill over from the hotel to stay at their house. And there was begun, twenty years ago, the first actual Alcoholics Anonymous group.

The number of them now is beyond count. Some say there

are 160,000 to 200,000 recovered alcoholics, but nobody knows how many extend beyond this into the fringes of the unknown. They say that each alcoholic holds within the orbit of his problem an average of fourteen persons who are affected by it. This means that conservatively two and a half million people's lives are different because of the existence of Alcoholics Anonymous. There is hardly a city or town or even hamlet now where you cannot find a group, strong and well-knit, or struggling in its infancy. Professor Austin Mc-Cormick of Berkeley, California, former Commissioner of Correction in the city of New York, who was also with us at the St. Louis Convention, said once in my hearing that AA may "prove to be one of the greatest movements of all time." That was years ago. Subsequently facts support his prophecy.

On the Sunday morning of the convention, I was asked to talk to them, together with Father Edward Dowling, S.J., a wonderful Roman Catholic priest who has done notable service for AA in interpreting it to his people, and Dr. Jim S., a most remarkable colored physician of Washington, on the spiritual aspects of the AA program. They are very generous to non-alcoholics, but I should have preferred that it be a bona fide alcoholic that did the speaking.

In the course of what I said to them, I remarked that I thought it had been wise for AA to confine its activity to alcoholics. But, I added, "I think we may see an effect of AA on medicine, on psychiatry, on correction, on the ever-present problem of human nature, and not least on the Church. AA indirectly derived much of its inspiration from the Church. Now perhaps the time has come for the Church to be re-awakened and re-vitalized by those insights and practices found in AA."

I think some of you may be a little horrified at this suggestion. I fear you will be saying to yourself, "What have we,

who have always been decent people, to learn from a lot of
reconstructed drunks?" And perhaps you may thereby reveal to yourself how very far you are from the spirit of Christ
and the Gospel, and how very much in need of precisely the
kind of check-up that may come to us from AA. If I need a
text for what I say to you, there is one ready to hand in
I Corinthians 1:26 ". . . God chose what is foolish in the
world to shame the wise, God chose what is weak in the
world to shame the strong." I need not remind you that
there is a good deal of sarcasm in that verse; because it must
be evident that anything God can use is neither foolish nor
weak, and that if we consider ourselves wise and strong, we
may need to go to school to those we have called foolish and
weak.

The first thing I think the Church needs to learn from AA
is that nobody gets anywhere till he recognizes a clearly-
defined need. These people do not come to AA to get made
a little better. They do not come because the best people are
doing it. They come because they are desperate. They are
not ladies and gentlemen looking for a religion, they are
utterly desperate men and women in search of redemption.
Without what AA gives, death stares them in the face. With
what AA gives them, there is life and hope. There are not a
dozen ways, there are not two ways, there is one way; and
they find it or perish. AA's, each and all, have a definite,
desperate need. They have the need, and they are ready to
tell somebody what it is if they see the least chance that it
can be met.

Is there anything as definite for you or me, who may happen not to be alcoholics? If there is, I am sure that it lies in
the realm of our conscious withholding of the truth about
ourselves from God and from one another, by pretending
that we are already good Christians. Let me here quote a
member of AA who has written a most amazing book. His

name is Jerome Ellison, and the book is *Report to the Creator*. In this he says, "The relief of being accepted can never be known by one who never thought himself unaccepted. I hear of 'good Christian men and women' belonging to 'fine old church families.' There were no good Christians in the first church, only sinners. Peter never let himself or his hearers forget his betrayal in the hour the cock crew. James, stung by the memory of his years of stubborn resistance, warned the church members: 'Confess your faults to one another.' That was before there were fine old church families. Today the last place where one can be candid about one's faults is in church. In a bar, yes, in a church, no. I know; I've tried both places." Let that sting you and me just as it should, and make us miserable with our church Pharisaism till we see it is just as definite and just as hideous as anybody's drunkenness can ever be, and a great deal more really dangerous.

The second thing the Church needs to learn from AA is that men are redeemed in a life-changing fellowship. AA does not expect to let anybody who comes in stay as he is. They live for nothing else but to extend and keep extending that help. Like the Church, they did not begin in glorious Gothic structures, but in houses or caves in the earth,—wherever they could get a foot-hold, meet people, and gather. It never occurs to an AA that it is enough for him to sit down and polish his spiritual nails all by himself, or dust off his soul all by himself, or spend a couple of minutes praying each day all by himself. His soul gets kept in order by trying to help other people get their souls in order, with the help of God. At once a new person takes his place in this redeeming, life-changing fellowship. He may be changed today, and out working tomorrow—no long, senseless delays about giving away what he has got. He's ready to give the little he has the moment it comes to him. The fellowship that re-

deemed him will wither and die unless he and others like
him get in and keep that fellowship moving and growing by
reaching others. Recently I heard an AA say that he could
stay away from his Veterans' meeting, his Legion, or his
Church, and nobody would notice it. But if he stayed away
from his AA meeting, his telephone would begin to ring the
next day!

"A life-changing fellowship" sounds like a description of
the Church. It is of the ideal Church. But the actual? Not
one in a hundred is like this. The laymen say this is the minister's job, and the ministers say it is the evangelist's job,
and everybody finds a rationalized excuse for not doing
what every Christian ought to be doing, i.e., bringing other
people into the redeeming, life-changing fellowship.

The third thing the Church needs to learn from AA is the
necessity for definite personal dealing with people. AA's
know all the stock excuses—they've used them themselves
and heard them a hundred times. All the blame put on someone else—my temperament is different—I've tried it and it
doesn't work for me—I'm not really so bad, I just slip a little
sometimes. They've heard them all, and know them for the
rationalized pack of lies they are. They constitute, taken together, the Gospel of Hell and Failure. I've heard them
laboring with one another, now patient as a mother, now
savage as a prize-fighter, now careful in explanation, now
pounding in a heavy personal challenge, but always knowing
the desperate need and the sure answer.

Are we in the Church like that? Have you ever been
drastically dealt with by anybody? Have you ever dared to
be drastic in love with anybody? We are so official, so polite,
so ready to accept ourselves and each other at face value. I
went for years before ever I met a man that dared get at
my real needs, create a situation in which I could be honest
with him, and hold me to a specific Christian commitment

and decision. One can find kindness and even good advice in the Church. That is not all men need. They need to be helped to face themselves as they really are. The AA people see themselves just as they are. I think many of us in the Church see ourselves as we should like to appear to others, not as we are before God. We need drastic personal dealing and challenge. Who is ready and trained to give it to us? How many of us have ever taken a "fearless moral inventory" of ourselves, and dared make the depth of our need known to any other human being? This gets at the pride which is the hindrance and sticking-point for so many of us, and which, for most of us in the Church, has never even been recognized, let alone faced or dealt with.

The fourth thing the Church needs to learn from AA is the necessity for a real change of heart, a true conversion. As we come Sunday after Sunday, year after year, we are supposed to be in a process of transformation. Are we? The AA's are. At each meeting there are people seeking and in conscious need. Everybody is pulling for the people who speak, and looking for more insight and help. They are pushed by their need. They are pulled by the inspiration of others who are growing. They are a society of the "before and after," with a clear line between the old life and the new. This is not the difference between sinfulness and perfection, but it is the difference between accepted wrong-doing and the genuine beginning of a new way of life.

How about us? Again I quote Jerome Ellison, in his report to God: ". . . I began to see that many of the parishioners did not really want to find You, because finding You would change them from their habitual ways, and they did not want to endure the pain of change . . . For our churchman-like crimes of bland, impenetrable pose, I offer shame . . ." I suppose that the sheer visibility of the alcoholic problem creates a kind of enforced honesty; but surely if we are ex-

posed again and again to God, to Christ, to the Cross, there
should be a breaking down of our pride and unwillingness
to change. We should know by now that this unwillingness,
multiplied by thousands and tens of thousands, is what is the
matter with the Church, and what keeps it from being what
God means it to be on earth. The change must begin somewhere. We know it ought to begin in us.

One of the greatest things the Church should learn from
AA is the need people have for an exposure to living Christian experience. In thousands of places, alcoholics (and
others) can go and hear recovered alcoholics speak about
their experiences and watch the process of new life and out-
look take place before their eyes. There you have it, the need
and the answer to the need, right before your eyes. They say
that their public relations are based, not on promotion, but
on attraction. This attraction begins when you see people
with problems like your own, hear them speaking freely of
the answers they are finding, and realize that such honesty
and such change is exactly what you need yourself.

No ordinary service of worship in the Church can possibly do this. We need to supplement what we do now by
the establishment of informal companies where people who
are spiritually seeking can see how faith takes hold in other
lives, how the characteristically Christian experience comes
to them. Some churches are doing this, but not nearly
enough of them. One I know where on Sunday evenings laymen and women speak simply about what has happened to
them spiritually: it is drawing many more by attraction. This
needs to be multiplied by the tens of thousands, and the
Church itself awakened.

As I looked out over that crowd of five thousand in Kiel
Auditorium in St. Louis, I said to myself, "Would that the
Church were like this—ordinary men and women with great
need who have found a great Answer, and do not hesitate

to make it known wherever they can—a trained army of enthusiastic, humble, human workers whose efforts make life a different thing for other people!"

Let us ask God to forgive our blindness and laziness and complacency, and through these re-made people to learn our need for honesty, for conversion, for fellowship and for honest witness!

"We can see the crucial importance of the great men of the past, but what of the present? Suppose Bill W. had not accepted the role today of an inspired messenger to alcoholics?"

From
"What Voices Do You Listen To?"
By
Samuel Moor Shoemaker

(From letter to S. M. S. from E. G.)
Chilhowie, Va.
November 15, 1959
Dear Sam:

About a week ago you sent to me a bundle of sermons left over from your mailings of "This Week's Word." I put them out on the prescription counter of my drug store. My customers pick them up while waiting for service, and one tells another of them. We have many requests for more as people are grateful to have them, and we have none left.

Can you send us more of any you happen to have? We can use as many as you can spare.

The one that is asked for most often is "What the Church has to learn from Alcoholics Anonymous," so we can use any amount of this one you have.

Thanks, Sam, for what you have done for your "hard-shelled" Methodist friend in Virginia.

                                        Gratefully,
                                        E. G.

(From letter written to Mrs. C. C. O. by Mr. E. G., after "Dr. S." died)

                                        Chilhowie, Va.
                                        September 30, 1963

Dear Mrs. O:

Thank you for your letter telling of Sam's death. I had not heard that he had died, and feel that his death is a very great loss to the Church, and really to America. I have always known that this man was one of the outstanding Christians of our time. Sam's death is a great personal loss.

When Sam was in New York, I saw him two or three times a year as I always stayed at Calvary House there, which was a part of Sam's parish and many stayed there, and Sam was always accessible to those who needed him. It was Sam who showed me, both by his words and his life, what complete dedication to God could mean, and he helped me to try to practice what he lived.

Once after he came to Pittsburgh, and sent "This Week's Word" to me each week, I put a number of these sermons out where my customers could take them. I remember especially one salesman who came into my store, who was an alcoholic, and who read Sam's sermon on "What the Church can Learn from Alcoholics Anonymous." This sermon was the cause of his looking up an A.A. group, and now he is one of the most enthusiastic Christians I ever knew. He took this sermon to a big convention in Chicago, and the manager of the Conrad Hilton Hotel there read it, and ordered 5,000 reprints made to be distributed from his front registration desk. They were just there for any who might pick them up, and I've often wondered how many this sermon helped.

I thought this story might interest you. Thanks again for writing to me.

Sincerely,
E. G.

(From letter to Canon Shoemaker from I. N.)

St. Petersburg, Florida
December, 1960

Dear Dr. Shoemaker:

I must express my gratitude to you for the help "This Week's Word" has brought to my life. I am an alcoholic, and a member of A.A. in good standing. I achieved my sobriety more than three years ago, and your sermons have helped me keep sober more than anything else I have found. Just to have these sermons on hand at my needed times, is a great source of strength and I read them again and again.

I have passed the one about the Church and A.A. to many of my friends who have the same problem, and it helps them, as it did me, when I first read it. Have you any spare copies? Mine is worn thin from handling.

May God bless you for your wisdom and help to us in A.A.

Gratefully,
I. N.

(From letter written to Mrs. C. C. O. from Mrs. Gertrude Behanna (Elizabeth Burns), author of *The Late Liz*, after Dr. Shoemaker died.)

"Burnside"
Stevenson, Md.
February 10, 1964

Dear C:

As you see, I am here at Sam's beloved "Burnside" for two days, between speaking engagements at the University of South Carolina, and Johns Hopkins University.

I am glad you are doing this job on Sam's great sermons; a job both for people and for Christ.

Yes, Sam and I loved one another. And while his supply of love was unlimited, it was not often personal. I think Sam and I had two rare and tremendous gifts in common; we had the *same* Christ, and the same sense of humor . . . and oh, so important this! 'Tis rare to have both the Spirit and the human in common. Too few both love *and* like each other, as we did.

When I think of Sam, I remember that he was a controversial priest. He offended the Pharisees, the stuffed shirts, the frightened, yet at the same time, he brought more humans to their knees before their Lord and his, than any ten men I ever knew.

Good luck with your book.

Love,
Gert

(From letter to Mrs. C. C. O. from Bill W., Co-founder of Alcoholics Anonymous)

New York, N.Y.
February 25, 1964

Dear Mrs. O:

Most certainly I share all of your gratitude for Sam and his great works. He is quite as much a founder of A.A. as any of us could be. Sam had a great love for A.A., and even those new members of A.A. who never heard him speak, have written to us of their sadness at his death. It is a great loss to all of us. Yet, how fortunate we are to have had him as long as we did.

Wishing you great success in publication of Sam's work.

Sincerely and with gratitude,
Bill W.

CHAPTER 4

GOD AND AMERICA

"We must not forget what God has done for America. We have been recipients of the choicest bounties of Heaven. We have been preserved these many years in peace and prosperity. We have grown in numbers, wealth and power as no other nation has ever grown. But we have forgotten God. Intoxicated with unbroken success, we have become too self-sufficient to feel the necessity of redeeming and preserving grace, too proud to pray to God who made us."

Abraham Lincoln

The longer I live the more fascinated do I become with the relation between our inherited faith and our enjoyment of freedom in the Western world. They seem to be connected as cause and effect.

Christianity, taking its rise on the edge of the East, moved westward and had its chief effect in Europe. We think of our propensity to war, and the still unsolved problems of our Western nations, and they certainly exist; but we must not forget that most of what civilizing influence we received came from the Christian religion. The dynamic which seems to be at the heart of the West, and to differentiate us from the lethargic East, has too often issued in strife and war; but it has also issued in progress, in greater opportunities for ordinary people, and especially in the belief that the freedom

men desire in their hearts can and should be achieved, for
them and for all others. One doubts whether the average
man, laboring under the almost universal condition of something approaching slavery, would ever have had the courage
to hope for liberty to help determine his own destiny, without some of the qualities Christianity has engendered in him.

Religious Concept of Freedom

It takes a great deal of courage to envision the throwing
off of long-standing shackles. Freedom can only come, I
think, or long remain in men, when they have some basic
belief about themselves as the children of God. What kept
hope in the minds of the Jews when they were in Egypt
or Babylon—what gave hope and patience to the Negroes
here in America—if it was not their profound religious conviction and orientation? Long before men talked as if they
"deserved" freedom, I think they were feeling that freedom
was something God intended them to have. The religious
conception of freedom is two-sided: it arises out of the awareness of being the children of God, and therefore having a
certain inherent dignity; but it must be preserved by an
equal accountability to Him in our use and stewardship of
it. If men who hold their liberty under God use the word
"rights" in connection with it, they also use with equal fre-
quency the word "responsibility."

Secular Concept of Freedom

We all know that there is another strain in our inherited
liberty in the West. It is the view of liberty associated with
the French Revolution. It is a purely humanistic, secularistic
thing, with its roots in the demands of men for freedom,
rather than in a view of it which takes it as a religious thing.
We must not take too low a view of this; historically this
view of liberty has sometimes been a good ally of our own

religious view. But liberty's dangers most often appear when one views it as simply a natural right, without also remembering its religious sanctions and responsibilities. Thomas Jefferson said, "I have sworn upon the altar of God eternal hostility against every form of tyranny over the mind of man." This is a noble ideal, Mr. Jefferson, but with it must go an equal concern for responsibility, else man will certainly abuse his great gift of freedom. We must also swear hostility towards all those forms of irresponsibility and self-indulgence which undermine freedom.

The great Frenchman de Tocqueville said, in his *Democracy in America*, "Democracy encourages a taste for physical gratification; this taste, if it becomes excessive, soon disposes men to believe that all is matter only; and materialism, in its turn, hurries them on with mad impatience to these same delights; such is the fatal circle within which democratic nations are driven round. It were well that they should see the dangers and hold back." And Dr. Russell Kirk, in his book *The Conservative Mind* (Henry Regnery Co., Chicago), says that "Tocqueville felt that the materialism which democracy encourages may so far obsess the public consciousness as to stifle, in all but a few independent souls, the ideas of freedom and variety." What perception the great Frenchman had, writing a century ago, and how accurately he forsaw the directions in which we would steer! These things, if not regarded and corrected, can be our undoing.

Religion and the American Way

Our great American fault and danger is to think that we have, as John Dewey once said, "discovered perpetual motion in politics." The "American way of life," indefinable as it is, works pretty well on the whole; but it is too formless and chaotic not to invite strong hands to invade it with increasing measures of control, unless we can manage to transfer from age to age the subtle spirit which must lie behind it—the spirit of fair play, the spirit of believing all men to be of worth, the spirit (rough and vague but real) of the Christian belief about man. The two-party political system is a good check here. Much better is the general spirit of religion, with responsibility at its heart as well as rights.

All this puts a sharp point on what we are doing in Church. We are here primarily to worship God. We are not here to flee from the world into a realm of make-believe where we can forget the daily grind and burden and decision of common life. Rather we are to bring these things in here with us, and ask God for His light upon them. Unless we do this, we shall increasingly have a religion that is selfish, aloof from life, sentimental and rarified; and we shall increasingly have a common life that is secular, materialistic, dog-eat-dog, and godless. People who do not expose themselves and their children regularly to religious influence are not only depriving them of the strengths and insights of personal faith, but they are robbing the nation of the kind of persons it most needs—men and women who hold their citizenship and exercise it as stewards under God, mindful all the while of something more than their own selfish interests.

Listen to this wise word from Whittaker Chambers concerning our time, "It is the first century since life began when a decisive part of the most articulate section of mankind has not merely ceased to believe in God, but has deliberately rejected God. And it is in this century in which this religious rejection has taken a specifically political form, so that the characteristic experience of the mind in this age is a political experience. At every point, religion and politics interlace, and must do so more acutely as the conflict between the two great camps of men—those who reject and those who worship God—becomes irrepressible. Those camps are not only outside, but also within nations."

The "West" Is Not the Kingdom

We must at all costs avoid the old pitfall of "using" God for our own ends and whipping up interest in religion solely because it is a safeguard of human freedom. Men have been Christians, and are being Christians today, in slave-labor camps and under the most repressive bondage human devilry can think up: some of the Church's "finest hours" have been in the catacombs. Moreover, we do not have perfection in our Western civilization, and must never identify our way of life with the Kingdom of God. We certainly must try, when we take our Christianity to other lands, to strip it of those Western elements which happen to have attached themselves to our version of Christianity. We must sow the seed of faith, and let the Spirit of God make of it what He will in other races and peoples.

But we must not forget what God has done for America. We must not confuse our own special kind of dynamic, much of it materialistic and selfish, with Christianity, though I believe the liveliness of this is owing principally to the Christian heritage. We must, however, hold fast to our awareness that religion and democracy are near allied. To quote de Tocqueville again, he once said, "Americans combine the notions of Christianity and liberty so intimately in their minds that it is impossible to make them conceive the one without the other."

Liberty and Control

The great problem of human liberty is the problem of inward and voluntary control. Liberty is license in the hands of people without moral and spiritual convictions. America today is almost hog-wild with its unrestrained liberty and its vast material wealth. I believe that the surest guarantee against further outward control, government or otherwise, is a greater measure of self-imposed restraint. Edmund Burke said that the less control there was within, the more there must be without. His half-brother wrote of John Randolph, "We very much doubt if he ever became a convert to the views of Burke, until the events of the last four years of Mr. Jefferson's administration led him to suspect that there may be something in the enjoyment of liberty, which soon disqualified a people for that self-government, which is but another name for freedom." So it may come about that the indulgence of freedom to satisfy ourselves, as over against the employment of freedom to obey God, may itself be a form of freedom's destruction.

Thus man needs a master. If he is not to have a fellowman for a master, with all the harm that comes both to tyrant and to slave in such a relation, he must accept a Master Whose lordship is always just, and always beneficent, while often running counter to human desires. In this strange world, good things can rot and go to seed. God gives man the desire and the potential for freedom. Man takes the freedom into his own hands and uses it for his own selfish ends. This may mean incipient slavery if he does not take care. Nothing else in this world is powerful enough to withstand the human ego but God.

Democracy and Humility

One of the reasons why Christianity is so essential to democracy is that humility is inherent in it. Nothing but his own awareness of God can keep a man from solemn and pompous estimates of himself. Nothing else can enable him to laugh at his own pretensions and self-importance. This is one of the things that makes totalitarians and dictators so frightfully dangerous: they never can laugh, least of all at themselves. To live in a democracy, one must know what true liberality is. A person who is genuinely liberal, and lis-

tens for what truth may be in a man who thinks in terms unlike his own, and even contrary to his own, must have the
humor that is closely akin to humility. One of the reasons
why we manage to live together in the midst of such great
disagreements and tensions is that our religion keeps remind-
ing us of the partial nature of all our most cherished beliefs,
and of our poor approximation of our most dearly-held ideals.
This should not create in us skepticism concerning our own
faith, but rather humility in the exercise of it. The best kind
of "order" in a nation is the somewhat free order of a home
where parents are both respected and loved. We must have
governments to establish justice; but real "order" can be
superimposed by no man—only by God. The more we are
concerned with trying to obey God, the less shall we live
in such a way as must soon or late invite human controls to
be set upon us. The more we are humble before the absolute
Good of God, the more we shall encourage the partial good
in ourselves and in others, without ever making it idolatrous
through pride.

Responsible Religion

Our Christianity needs to be personal—very personal. It
needs to be lived out within the limited democracy of the
Church, and of a church. But it must always be aware of
its responsibility for the nation. We ought to love America,
being grateful for the best in her, and continually asking
God for His will concerning our nation. Freedom is essen-
tially freedom to obey God. If we persist in using our freedom to ignore Him, we may eventually find freedom has
eluded us altogether. These temporal blessings are still blessings from Christ, and we cannot think of them wholly apart
from Him.

One day I was flying east and looked down upon a crazy-
quilt of a town somewhere in New Jersey. There were hovels

and fine houses, streets and mudpaths, mingled in great disorder. But in the middle of that town there was a church, brick with white trim, well-built and orderly. It stood out as a symbol of voluntary order in a chaotic town. So must the church be the island of order and sanity and faith from which our society takes its pattern.

Let us strive and work and pray that this church and all churches may be the true leaven of this nation!

"History is cluttered with the wreckage of nations that became indifferent to God and died."
From
Witness
By
Whittaker Chambers

(From letter to S.M.S. from S. M.)

Philadelphia, Pa.
February 18, 1961
Dear Dr. Shoemaker:

Is there a possibility that I can have 100 copies of your sermon, "God and America" to distribute to my friends? What you say about Christians being vanguards to awaken America to our perils and responsibilities is so clearly put that I covet for my friends what this sermon has done for me.

Indeed, the way you manage in all you say to help people translate spiritual truth into practical action is so needed today, that I have found courage to ask what may be impossible. I'll be glad to pay for the sermons. Please send me what you can spare, and I promise to see that they are well used.

Thank you in advance for this favor, and thank you for all you have meant to me and other members of my church.

Faithfully,

S. M.

(From letter to S. M. S. from M.M.)

New York, N. Y.

December 1, 1961

Dear Dr. Shoemaker:

I have thanked you before, but this last one, "God and America" calls for another letter. Of all your sermon themes, those which stress the bond between the faith we inherit and the freedoms we enjoy are my favorites; and this one says it all.

If I may say so, I know of no other preacher who sounds this note so insistently and so well.

I do appreciate the way you give us in your sermons such practical tips about how to accomplish the difficult business of being, or trying to be, better Christians in our everyday lives. I wish the thousands who already receive "This Week's Word" could be multiplied many, many times.

Sincerely,

M. M.

CHAPTER 5

DANGER AHEAD UNLESS—

"Surely God must have an answer to our time in which the danger is, obviously, the destruction of freedom throughout the world, through the destruction of faith in God."
From
God's Answer to Our Time
By
Samuel Moor Shoemaker

The season of Advent which begins today has always been one both of gladness and of solemnity—gladness, because we look forward to the coming of our Lord at Christmas in mercy and redemption; solemnity, because we look forward to His coming again in glory and in judgment. This is a period, perhaps even more than Lent, for the most serious heart-searching, for we do it now, not as an exercise in personal discipline, but as an act of self-appraisal and of world-appraisal in the light of the Judgment of God.

God's Laws

We are so disinclined in these days to hear anything about God except His mercy and love that we wince when somebody says "judgment." But if this world is something like a school, judgment is something like examinations. The Last

Judgment seems to me a little like a Final Examination. We have been taking tests and examinations all along; there will be a final one that covers the whole course. If life means anything, if we are meant to learn something here, if God has established moral laws, in fact if there be a God at all, I do not see how we can do away with the reality of Judgment. In Christ, God seeks to redeem,. and love is the essence of His nature. But God is holy, and He expects obedience from us. No true love is all softness and comfort. Love has its expectations and its austerities. Therefore there must always be in true religion a warning note. And men of God are false to their commission if they are not prepared to speak it.

The situation today is so complex, the factors are so numerous and often so conflicting, that only a very wise man would dare raise his voice in anything like an authoritative way. But all of us can and must try to look the facts in the face and try to understand something of what is taking place about us.

Some Alarming Facts

Many have called attention to the fact that, while there seems to be some increase of interest in religion and church-going, there has been a serious increase also in crime, delinquency and general moral indifference.

A vice-president of a large company that is in the business of underwriting bankers and their tellers says that dishonesty is increasing at such an alarming rate in the nation that they are scared to death: they are in process of increasing their rates, but see no way to end the deterioration.

A writer in the *New York Times Magazine* makes the point about the Van Doren case that a teacher is a special guardian of truth, and faults the academic system which taught both the teacher and the students who defended him. He says that a society which condemned what Van Doren did would also have to condemn itself, and this it is unwilling to do; he calls this "a moral obtuseness which signifies the beginning of the end of civilized society." All of us are sinners and must always remember Christ's word about "he that is without sin"; but this was never meant to condone evil, only to seek the redemption of the evildoer, be this ourselves or another.

Our people are often careless of their political responsibilities. A congressman said that in his state the number of people who voted in 1896 was 80 percent; in 1958 this percentage fell to an all-time low of 20 percent. Someone disputed him on this, and told him a check would reveal a much higher percentage. He made the check and found the actual number was in the neighborhood of 10 percent. An engeneer friend of mine says the troublemakers go to the polls and the good people stay home and watch TV.

Syd Harris has lately had some rather alarming things to say about adolescent delinquents, and declares that by the time a boy has reached 16, little can be done to remove the hate and ferocity that infect his feelings. He says prevention is the only treatment that makes sense, but says that "parents lack either the intelligence, the will or the money to cope" with the problem. "Meanwhile society becomes a mass-victim of this disease."

Surely the people of this city need no reminder of the full-scale tragedy of a strike. Freedom demands the right of men to strike for their protection; but what has freedom to say to labor overlords whose pride and power count for more than the welfare of the men and their families? And has not labor taken its cue directly from a management that is all too determined that their own pride and power shall not be infringed? Millions of people are affected adversely by delay in reaching a settlement that one day simply must be reached. Neither side seems willing to forgo some of its

pride for the benefit of society, the nation or our place in
the world.

Allen Dulles, former Director of Central Intelligence,
warned us that the Soviet Union is increasing its production
at a rate far higher than ours, and concentrating it upon
military, economic and political warfare. Their living standard is about one quarter of ours, but their investment in
industry this year about equals ours. We must greatly speed
up our own economic growth better to serve the needs of
national survival.

A writer in *Christianity and Crisis* calls ethics "obsolete."
He says, "The sentimentalist buries morals in a mud-bath of
maudlin compassion. The analytic philosopher assists by
proving that it is all emotive anyway. The psychotherapists
and the sociologists carefully skirt the use of ethical categories. The theologian puts morals out of sight by burying
them under ground, by elevating them to the skies, or by
dissipating them into the self or into society. The sophisticate
views the whole affair with contempt. And the respectable
chap, even when he conforms, is at heart a cultural relativist."

Sir Charles Darwin, grandson of his great namesake and
himself a most distinguished scientist, says that the world's
population in 50 years will be five billion, about double what
it is now. The present population explosion is going to mean
a shortage of food some day, and especially a shortage in
fresh water. Sea water is of little help far inland. Many baths
can be a thing of the past. Sir Charles thinks we are living
in "the absolute golden age of the world." The inevitable
overcrowding means the absolute necessity for some kind
of population control. Our own population is increasing
dangerously fast. Here, surely, is one of the major human
problems of our time.

The Gravest Fact of All

And I think it is closely related to another grave problem which we must now face together. The Western world of Europe and North America is a small minority of the world's population. The so-called "white race" is about one-fifth of the human race—the rest are brown, red or black-skinned. But in the white races is gathered most of the world's wealth. The *Living Church* of Nov. 22, 1959 reprinted from a paper in England this statement:

"Today, the western world stands trial for cruelty by wilful neglect. This is the evidence: Two-thirds of the world are underfed—at least 1660 million people. Two-thirds of the world are dead by 30. Half the world lives on rice—and little else. Most of the world's 900 million are undernourished. And the indictment: the 19 richest countries have just over one-sixth of the world's people and two-thirds of the world's income."

In the remarkable statement from Dr. Henry Smith Leiper which is reprinted at the end of this chapter he reduces this all to a picture easily visualized. If we compressed the world's population of two and a half billion into a community of a thousand living in one town, sixty of these people would represent the present U.S.; the rest would be represented by 940 people. The 60 Americans would be receiving half the total income; the other 940, the other half; 330 people would be called Christians, 670 would not. Less than 100 would be Protestants, more than 230 would be Roman Catholics, 80 would be Communists, and 370 under Communist domination. Less than a third would be white, more than two-thirds non-white. The Americans would average a life expectancy of 70; the rest, under 40. The 60 Americans would have 15 times as many possessions per person as all the rest of the people. They would produce 16 percent of the

total food supply, but consume only 1.5 percent of it, keeping the remainder in storage. The 940 non-Americans would
always be hungry, while we Americans eat 72 percent above
maximum food requirements. We could save money by
giving away most of what we store. Except for the 200 more
favored people, mostly of the West, the others would be
ignorant, poor, hungry and sick. Half could not read nor
write. Half the people in this group of a thousand would
never have heard of Jesus Christ; but more than half would
be hearing about Marx, Lenin, Stalin, and Khrushchev. The
average American Christian family would be spending,
through taxes, about $850 a year for military defense and
less than $4 a year to share their Christian faith with others
in the community. Out of an average of $2,500 per year, the
gift of each American for all purpose outside private and
personal gifts would average less than $55 a year, or about
$4.50 a month.

Dereliction and Danger

One has only to contemplate these things in this visual
fashion to realize how they look from our own standpoint, if
we call ourselves Christians; and then how they look from
the standpoint of the rest of the world much of which does
not call itself Christian. Not only have we been derelict in
our duty, but nothing gives the Communists a better talking-
point than this obvious, inescapable fact. We are certainly
not doing what we should, and our refusal to look these facts
in the face, to be disturbed about them, and to set about
some appropriate action in face of them constitutes a patent
danger. A wealthy suburb surrounded by blighted and
underprivileged areas is not only a moral anomaly from a
Christian standpoint, it is a dangerous situation for the
wealthy suburb.

What can and should we do? God is in human events, and

human events today are judging us in the over-privileged West. Nothing stands still. Injustice and unfairness, cruelty and indifference, do not remain forever. Something is going to have to give. We must act or events will act upon us. This is as clear as daylight.

Let's Be Realistic

First, I think, we can look the perhaps unpleasant facts in the face, and take a long, unevasive stare at them. We have for so long lived with the idea that some of us were privileged and most of us were poor, and that this state of things has existed for a long time. But this rests on a foundation of assumed security which grows less dependable all the time. The inherent wrong of the situation is aggravated by what the Communists, and all who are anti-West, can truthfully say about the sins of the West. We feel the annoyance of a headline, then turn to the pursuit of our life and our job. The gravity of the situation seems to be hard to exaggerate. Admiral Moreell said that it is hard to convince people who are comfortable that they are in danger. We must stop pretending that matters are better than they appear. Let us be realistic about our situation.

We CAN Act

Second, let us face the fact that dangerous situations are created by people, and the danger can be relieved by people. We are not helpless pawns in the hands of the impersonal forces of Fate. Once intelligent men see the danger fully, we can begin doing what is necessary to ward it off. If war were upon us, we would adjust our lives to its dangers and rigors knowing that everything else depends upon our retaining our freedom. We have been given plenty of time to see the situation. The trouble is some of us have gone to sleep watching its familiar and unwelcome outlines. If we fully realized the danger, we should gird ourselves to meet it adequately. But this danger must be met, not with strong armies and industries alone, but with mercy and humanity and the sharing of our blessings. We seem to find this harder than fighting a war.

We MUST Act

Third, I think this rich minority of a poor world is going to have to change its ways voluntarily, or its ways are going to be changed involuntarily; I do not think things will stay as they are, nor that the "haves" are going to accumulate more. Why do we have to live as luxuriously as we do? Why can we not cut down on what we spend for food, for clothes, for amusement, for needless comfort, while others starve, are cold, sick, hungry? We are much too easy on ourselves. Not many of us are deliberately wicked, but very many of us are trivial and irresponsible. Christ's warnings about money and wealth are on almost every page of the Gospels. If a starving man lay at our doorstep, we should probably do something about him. When millions of desperately poor people live near us in a shrinking world, why does not our compassion move us in the same way? We belong to a great material civilization. We have the technical knowledge to help the peoples of the underprivileged world. We must help them to slow down the explosion of population, but we must help them feed the children that are already here. If the Christians do not rise up and do something about this, I do not know who is going to do it. If it is not done, I think we shall be a nation and a civilization that has been weighed in the balance, and found wanting. In our Christian faith, God has not offered us a lovely, unselfish way of life that would be pleasant if everybody followed it: He has shown us the laws of life, laws as fixed and binding as any physical or chemical laws in the material world. We do not break them; if we go against them, they break us.

Let us heed the solemn words in this morning's lesson: "see that you do not refuse him who is speaking . . . For our God is a consuming fire."

"Then they also will answer, 'Lord, when did we see thee hungry or thirsty or a stranger or naked or sick or in prison, and did not minister to thee?' Then he will answer them, 'Truly, I say to you, as you did it not to one of the least of these, you did it not to me.' And they will go away into eternal punishment, but the righteous into eternal life."

Matthew 25:44-46, (RSV)

OUR WORLD IN MINIATURE

by
Henry Smith Leiper

If in our imagination we might compress the total population of the world, now more than two-and-a-half-billion persons, into a community of one thousand persons living in a single town, the following is a picture of the contrasts we would then vividly see:

Sixty persons would represent the present U.S. population; the rest of the world would be represented by 940 persons. The 60 Americans would be receiving half of the total income of the entire community; the 940 other persons would share the remaining half.

Of the Americans in the town, 36 would be members of Christian churches. and 24 would not. In the town as a whole, about 330 people would be classified as Christians, and 670 would not be so classified. Less than 100 in the whole community would be Protestant Christians, and more than 230 would be Roman Catholics. At least 80 people in the town would be believing Communists, and 370 others would be under Communist domination.

Classified as to skin color, 303 people would be white, and 697 would be classified as "non-white." The 60 Americans would have an average life expectancy of 70 years; all the other 940 would average under 40 years.

The 60 Americans would have 15 times as many possessions per person as all the rest of the people. On the average, they would produce 16 percent of the town's total food supply, but would consume all but 1.5 percent of what they raise and keep most of it for their own future use in expensive storage equipment. Since most of the 940 non-Americans in the community would always be hungry and would never quite know when they would get enough to eat, the situation created by this disparity in food supply and the existence of vast food reserves becomes readily apparent, particularly in view of the fact that Americans already eat 72 percent above the maximum food requirements. Because of the cost of storing their surplus food, they could actually save money by giving away any excess food; but many would regard that as the dangerous "give-away" program of soft-headed "do-gooders."

Of the community's total supply of electric power, the 60 Americans would have 12 times as much as all the rest; 22 times as much coal; 21 times as much oil and gasoline; 50 times as much steel; and 50 times as much in general equipment of all kinds. Of the 60 Americans, the lowest income groups would be better off than the average in much of the rest of the town.

With the exception of perhaps 200 persons representing Western Europe and a few favored classes in other areas, such as South America, South Africa, and Australia, and a few wealthy Japanese, literally most of the non-American people in this imaginary compressed community would be ignorant, poor, hungry, and sick—half of them would be unable to read or write.

Moreover, half of the people in this community would never have heard of Jesus Christ, or what He taught, and for what He lived and died. On the other hand, more than half would be hearing about Karl Marx, Nicolai Lenin, Joseph Stalin, Nikita Khrushchev, and other Communist leaders.

In view of these facts, it is interesting to contemplate that the average Christian American family would be indirectly (through taxes) spending at least $850 each year for military defense and less than four dollars a year to share their Christian faith with the rest of the people in the community.

Out of his average income of $2,500 per year, the gift of each American person for all purposes other than private and personal gifts would average less than $55 per year. This might raise a question as to how seriously he regards the Christian faith or the meaning of Christmas with the emphasis on peace on earth and good will among men.

(From letter written to Mrs. C. C. O. by G. L., ex-Communist writer, author of many books and articles which expose Communism)

New York, N.Y.
February 24, 1964

Dear Mrs. O:

Thank you for asking me to say a little of what Sam Shoemaker has meant in my life. It was my good fortune to go almost directly from the atmosphere of Communism into the atmosphere of living, organic Christianity, for I landed in Calvary Episcopal Church in New York where Sam Shoemaker was the Rector.

As I lived and worked in the Parish House there, I was in

constant touch with the dynamic positiveness of Sam's faith, and his love for Jesus Christ.

In striking contrast to the irresponsibles who unite wholesale with Communism, Sam was no pussy-footing collaborator. For example, one day before the Communists took over China, Sam sent me a letter from an organization that was raising money for the Chinese. His name was on the letterhead as one of the sponsors. I called Sam and told him that I knew without a doubt that the secretary of that organization was an important member of the Communist party, and that all money raised would go directly to the Communists. Next morning on my desk was a carbon copy of his letter of resignation from that group.

During 1949 and 1950 the Communists almost succeeded in destroying Whittaker Chambers. He was a friend of mine, and the one who helped free me from Communism.

Propaganda of the Party was so strong and so vicious and bitter that some spilled over on me, because I held out for the truth that Whittaker Chambers was telling the truth, and even risking everything he loved and valued most in life to witness for God and to his countrymen about Communism. No one believed me when I gave them facts; no one except Sam. And he never deviated from that belief.

Not long before his death he sent me a carbon copy of a letter he had written to the editor of a well-known journal, recommending my novel, "Full Circle" and he said to this editor, "It was Grace Lumpkin who set me right about Whittaker Chambers."

I mention this to show the measure of the man. Not the least of his bigness was his humility and willingness to listen to me even when I stood alone. It was no little thing he did for me at that time, and yet he ignored his part in it. "*I* was set right," he said.

Again I thank you for allowing me this part in Sam's book. I loved Sam dearly, and you have my grateful blessing.

G. L.

(From E. P. M. to Mrs. C. C. O. after Dr. Shoemaker died)

Evanston, Illinois
March 6, 1963

Dear Mrs. O:

Thank you for letting me know of your plan to put together a few of Dr. Shoemaker's sermons from "This Week's Word." I still use them. The one I remember best is "Danger Ahead Unless . . ." which I heard first on the radio one Sunday morning in 1960 when "Dr. Sam" was on the Episcopal Hour.

Later when I received this sermon in "This Week's Word" I wrote for additional copies, and each one went neatly into letters I wrote to those who I knew would profit most by this sermon.

I never heard Dr. Shoemaker speak except on the radio, but to me, he was not a voice, but a person. Someone I knew. When he spoke on the radio, it was as if he was in my living room.

I keep a batch of his sermons beside my night table, and read them often. Thus, "Dr. Sam" speaks to me now just as he did that first time I heard him give his "Danger Ahead Unless . . ." This sermon is of timeless value.

Thank you again.

Sincerely,
E. P. M.

PART TWO

JESUS CHRIST IS THE ANSWER

"There is a force loose in the world called faith. It is as palpable in its effects as electricity."

From
"Faith in Vital Energy"
By
Samuel Moor Shoemaker

CHAPTER 6

BELIEVE ALSO IN ME

"The very first obligation of a Christian is that he believe in his Lord and Savior, Jesus Christ. The distinctive thing in Christianity is always faith in Jesus Christ."

From
"Believing and Doing"
By
Samuel Moor Shoemaker

On this glorious day, when we remember the coming into the world of our Lord and Saviour Jesus Christ, let us consider some of the ways in which He has enlarged the world's faith. I ask you to think about some words of His that are pregnant with a richer meaning than perhaps we have ever seen in them, the familiar words with which the fourteenth chapter of St. John opens: "Let not your heart be troubled: ye believe in God, believe also in me."

Have you ever considered that this is a challenge to everyone to go further and deeper in their faith? It does not appear to be a simple imperative to believe in God, and in Christ: but rather to go the added distance of faith which begins with belief in God, but goes on to belief in Christ. Our Christian faith is founded on our belief in God: that is its groundwork and base. But Christianity is something beside a confirmation of our faith in God: it is an extension of our faith to faith in Christ, and this in turn affects our faith in God. "Ye believe in God, believe also in me." Let us look at some of the ways in which faith in Christ enlarges and enriches faith in God.

Christ and the Father

Ye believe in a primary Force, believe also in a Heavenly Father. There are actually very few atheists, and one comes to feel that a real unbelief in God arises from subjective emotions of an unhappy sort much more than from honest intellectual considerations. The average person moves from effect back to cause, and says that nothing as wonderful and orderly as this universe could merely "happen." The ordering of such a vast and law-abiding machine must require some kind of force. Christ comes saying to them, "Him whom you accept as a necessary postulate, Him I declare unto you as the Father of your spirits." Jesus believes that God is "personal." I don't know what that means to you; but to me it means that He thinks and He wills, He plans and He executes—that is what I mean by personality, a free agent that can imagine and foresee, and then execute and carry out. Jesus comes very insistently to our time with that increased faith, from Force to Father; because there are many in our time who believe in the Force but not in the Father. If we believe in Christ, we cannot believe in less than a personal God.

God as Helper

Ye believe in a God that is, believe also in a God that helps. We can hardly think at all except upon the postulate of some kind of God. Life does not even make sense, let alone come to a great significance, without that. But there are many who feel He is only background. It is as if He had given creation a primeval push, and then retired. Now He sits in celestial splendor, and watches the vast panorama roll along. Such a God may satisfy the mind, but can never satisfy the soul. We long for something more than this, whether there be more than this or not. Christ says there is more than this. "Your heavenly Father knoweth that we have need of all these things . . . Seek ye first His kingdom and His righteousness, and all these things shall be added unto you." The God, Who is the background to all of life, Christ believes to be the Helper of all life, also. God helps us who are physically but atoms in a vast space, but spiritually are His children, and need the touch of His hand, the warmth of His love, the inspiration by which He motions and guides us. We long for a God like this. Now Christ tells us that the God that is, is like this. You may have to take it on His authority until your own experience has confirmed it to you. When you pray, do not cling so to your own desires that you forget His desires; do not hug to yourself the heartache so closely that you give Him no chance to come in. Open yourself to God, the God in Whom Christ believes, the God Who helps: and He will help you.

God Revealed

Ye believe in a God invisible, believe also in a God Who reveals Himself. The vast impersonal force in which most persons believe, with little comfort or power resulting, is invisible. "Second Isaiah" knew God as any man of the prophets knew Him, yet even he says, "Verily thou art a God that hidest thyself." The Jews as a people were greatly conscious of Him. He was their God, and increasingly they saw that He was also the God of all the whole earth. But His complete spirituality, His superiority to any kind of form or body or manifestation (except in mighty works) was an axiom with them. It altered their thought profoundly to admit even the possibility of His coming in a human form. But we know now that the full revelation of God could come in no other way. We still feel a great "otherness" in God, as over against man: a transcendence, a holiness, a purity which is for us to look upon like the sun, blinding in its glory. But as men contemplated what had happened on Christmas, and what was the nature of Him Who walked here among us in the flesh, they said there was no other explanation: "The Word was made flesh" (John 1:14). The invisible God had revealed Himself. We are accustomed to the familiar words, "Have I been so long with you, and yet hast thou not known me, Philip? He that hath seen me hath seen the Father." But those words represent a revolution in thinking for a strict Jew; as they mean a revolution for us if we are to let our faith grow from believing in an invisible God to believing in a God Who has revealed Himself perfectly in the life of Jesus Christ, so that men will know and understand the nature of God.

God of Grace

Ye believe in a God of law, believe also in a God of grace. Our age does not have difficulty believing in a God of law: a God Who put law into this universe as we put steel into our buildings to give them shape and consistency and hold them together. We can go farther than that and admit that God is a God of moral law, also. As there are physical laws which to break mean physical disaster, so there are moral laws which to break mean moral disaster. A God of law seems to us reasonable, necessary. But St. John elsewhere gives us the greater truth: "The law was given by Moses, but grace and truth came by Jesus Christ" (John 1:17). That is, Moses showed men the holy demands which God made upon them, and it was a great step in human development. But men soon found there was a gap between them and the attainment of the aims of those moral laws. They needed power if they were to reach any such ideals. They needed forgiveness when they failed. I believe it true to say that the greatest contribution which Christ made to the inward, psychological harmony of man was His insistence on the availability of grace from God to enable us to meet the moral demands of God. The God Who expects righteousness of us sends us help to meet His holy demands.

God As Servant

Ye believe in a God Who is a King, believe also in a God Who is a servant. We must accept God's majesty if we accept His existence. It ought to give us believers in a democracy considerable anxiety to remember that, at least in two places—and very important ones—there is a simple, absolute monarchy: and that is, in heaven, and in the hearts of Christians. Perhaps our democracy will only work when we remember the larger autocracy which underlies it. There has been some very shallow thinking about a God Who was somehow struggling into being through His creation: that is simply not the Jewish-Christian teaching about God. When we sing of a God "who dwellest between the Cherubim," we are making a pictorial representation of a God of great majesty and awe. All this is forever true. But in Christ we see another complementary and enlarged truth. This God Who is the King came in Christ ". . . not to be ministered unto, but to minister" (Matthew 20:28), ". . . took upon him the form of a servant, and was made in the likeness of men" (Philippians 2:7). Part of the imperishable wonder of this day is the extraordinary contrast between God in the high heaven, and the Child in the manger. But these are not two; they are one. For it was always the nature of Almighty God to be a servant, to care for and protect and look after His children; but we did not dare to believe it until Christ came and showed it to us. What should this do to any pride we may have about serving others, whoever they are, whatever their needs, as if we were too good to do what Almighty God deigned to do?

God As Redeemer

Ye believe in a God Who is the Judge of all the earth, believe also in a God Who is the Redeemer of all mankind. The moment we admit a law, we admit a judgment as penalty for disobeying it, for that is the nature of law. There are truths of Christianity especially understood by particular generations, and one of the truths that we find no hesitancy whatever in accepting is this: "Be not deceived; God is not mocked: for whatsoever a man soweth, that shall he also reap" (Galatians 6:7). It means we cannot play fast and loose with moral law and not suffer for it. When a man persistently plays with the fire of sin, sooner or later, he is going to get burned. When you take chances among what you call the "doubtful" things, but push your conscience to one side when you do it, you may discover later on that there was no doubt about them at all. Law itself is merciless. It judges whether or no—and ignorance of it excuses no man, for ignorance of moral law generally means we would not listen to the warning whisper of conscience. Back of law is God, its Author and its Guardian. To Him we are accountable now, and shall be accountable in the end. That is the nature of God, of law, and of life. But that is not all there is to the nature of God. For God, being a Person, is merciful as abstract law cannot be. God being loving, intercepted between our wrongdoings and their full requital. He came into the world to be the world's Saviour, and on a cross He made atonement for the sins of the whole world. It is a great mystery how that part of God which is love made atonement to that other part of God which is law, and changed man's status before Him. It is a great spiritual fact, felt by all who have come under the Cross and its redeeming power, but almost impossible to state in intellectual terms without doing injustice to some part of God's nature and revelation. The important thing for us to remember is that law and love, judgment and redemption, are two sides of the same thing, different ways of understanding the same God, different ways of His manifesting Himself to the world. We are all subject to His law. But we are all privileged to share, if we will, in His redemption. This yearning, loving, redeeming side of God's nature—there from everlasting to everlasting—was made clear and unmistakeable to us in Christ. "Ye believe in God, believe also in me."

Yet what I have been saying to you may be open to mis-understanding. There has always been the risk of a false distinction between Jesus and God—as if God stood for all the hard things in religion, and Jesus for the gentle ones. This once made a child say, "I love Jesus, but I hate God." We shall misunderstand all this unless we realize that every-thing that Jesus was, God is also. It is our Christian faith that the Two are One and with the Holy Spirit form the Holy Trinity. There is a distinction of Persons but not a distinction of qualities. Jesus did not come to say these greater, more gracious, ·more gentle, more moving truths about God as it were on His own; He came revealing them for God the Father as well as about Him.

Jesus, the Way to the Father

But we must always seek the Father through Christ. Not only will our conceptions of God be vague and impersonal and perhaps even hard without the modification which Christ brings to us, but we cannot understand God without Christ. It is possible to "believe in" Him in the sense that we believe in His existence, without drawing near to Him, or knowing how to draw near to Him. Christ is both the Revelation of God, and the Avenue to Him. I find it hard to get in touch with Absolute and Almighty God: He is too great, too high, too different, too distant. But in Christ I see Him. Often I have used the illustration, but it serves better than any other. I stood in the Baptistry of St. John Lateran in Rome trying to look up and see the dark and ancient mosaics above my head. Then a guard thrust a little mirror into my hand, and looking down to see what it was, I saw the mosaics above my head perfectly reflected in the mirror in my hand. God is the mosaics high above us, and Christ is the mirror in our hands in which to see Him. It really is as simple as that.

"Ye believe in God, believe also in me."

God give us this Christmas day, and all our days—and give to all whom we love and from whom we may be separated—this deeper, richer Christian faith that was brought to us this glad day in the life of the Child of Bethlehem!

"Our lives should be islands of belief and, therefore of sanity in a sea of bewilderment and madness."

From
"What Christians Believe About Life"
By
Samuel Moor Shoemaker

(From letter to Mrs. C.C.O. from Dr. J. McT.)

Baltimore, Md.
March, 1964

Dear Mrs. O:

Thank you for your letter about Dr. Sam. I wish I could adequately put into words his influence, and the influence of his sermons, which we had each week. But I can comply with your request that I tell you why I wrote him that I considered T.W.W. the most important periodical which came to our home those two and a half years. It was because all of us read them, and because those sermons helped us live our lives day by day.

But, great as the sermons are, they were not as helpful to me as the memory of the few personal contacts I had with Dr. Sam at "Burnside." The one I remember best is that of a summer afternoon when he and I worked in his garden. Dr. Sam was working among the boxwood, and I was spreading mulch. As we worked Dr. Sam talked of his own practical approach to life, and of using his Christian faith in the problems which everyone meets, because of our seemingly unavoidable pressures. I asked him how he maintained such equanimity, and always seemed to have time for people, in face of the multiple interests he maintained.

"Well," he answered, "first I pray about what is on my mind, and then I try to implement prayer with action." Then, with his inimitable chuckle, he added, "Of course, I don't always do this, but when I am able to, pressures melt away."

It was Dr. Sam's *faith*, simple, strong and more real than most of us know anything about, that came through in his words. This was why I said what I did to him about "This Week's Word."

It is very difficult to put the sense and feeling of that afternoon into words, and what I have said does not express it at all adequately. But today, and as long as I live, I will draw on the memory of that afternoon and on Dr. Sam's faith and philosophy, even though my attempts to adopt his behavior are very poor.

I'm glad you are doing this collection, and do keep me in touch with progress. I can think of no better gift to give my friends than to give them Dr. Sam's book.

Thank you again for letting me know about the book, and Godspeed!

Cordially,
J. McT.

(From letter to the late Canon S. M. Shoemaker from Mrs. R. C. P.)

Bethesda, Md.
October, 1960

Dear Dr. Shoemaker:

Last summer as I sat alone on a bluff overlooking Lake Ontario, I found in my pocket the last sermon I had received before I left home. It was called, "How To Find God," and as I began to read I realized I had read a book, maybe another sermon, in which you said the same things.

Perhaps it was the beauty of that quiet place, and because I was alone, that the words had meaning I'd never found before in your words. But I like to think that that sermon was in my hands just that day because, so soon, very troublesome things were coming to us, when the faith I found that morning was to be so needed.

Anyway, I just wanted you to know that that sermon made all the difference in how my husband and I have been able to meet trouble about which we knew nothing that lovely summer day.

Thank you for sending "This Week's Word."

Gratefully,
(Mrs.) R. C. P.

CHAPTER 7

WHY I BELIEVE THAT JESUS IS GOD

"When you touch Jesus Christ you touch something like radium at the center of history. To discover this is like discovering a cure for cancer. To know a cure for cancer and not to release it would be a crime against humanity. We know Christ as a cure for the sickness of human nature, and not to release Him, this too, is a great selfishness and evil."

From
The Experiment of Faith
By
Samuel Moor Shoemaker

"Thou art the Christ, the Son of the living God."
Matthew 16:16

Christianity claims to be the true revelation of God. It claims to be unique. It recognizes and welcomes truth as it may be found in other religions, but while these may have partial apprehensions of truth, Christianity claims to be the truth. It therefore claims the allegiance of all men, and is engaged in an ageless enterprise to reclaim the souls and convince the minds and touch the hearts of all men everywhere. If this sounds dogmatic, remember that truth is always dogmatic, for two opposite theories cannot both be true. You cannot cause two and two to equal five, no matter how liberal may be your attitude. You cannot escape the dogma that a straight line is the shortest distance between two points. And while men's apprehensions of the truth may vary, the truth toward which their minds aspire does not vary. If it did, we should have no such thing as truth. Truth itself implies uniqueness. If, amid all the human search for God, it should prove to be the case that once God came down and searched for man, that would be unique and it would be truth for religion, as other things are truth for mathematics or physics or geometry.

Religion—Not "A" Religion

The uniqueness of the claim of Christianity—its claim that it is not "a" religion but Religion with a capital R, lies in the conviction that Jesus was the divine Son of God, in an unique sense. All of us have in us a potential spark of divinity, for we are made in the image of God. Theoretically I suppose there is nothing to say that we might not progress until that spark had become a consuming flame; but all that is mere theory, while it is the Christian faith that in Jesus this was not theory but fact, not remote possibility but present reality. Why have people believed that and what reasons are there for it?

There can be no doubt that the men immediately about Him came to the inescapable conclusion that He was the Son of God in this unique sense. Remember, He was born amongst a people with a horror of idolatry, and idolatry was any confusion of a created thing with the Creator; so they were predisposed by history and training to believe that only God could be God, and that no man could ever be God. Yet, when He had been with His closest associates for a time, He asked them one day whom men said that He was; and they replied, "Some say John the Baptist, others Elijah, or Jeremiah, or one of the prophets." "But whom say ye that I am," He asked. And Peter, presumably speaking for them all (and if he had not been so speaking there would surely have ensued a dispute), "Thou art the Christ, the Son of the living God" (Matthew 16:14-16).

A Parallel

We are so accustomed to this that the wonder of it escapes us. Suppose a young itinerant preacher should set about a spiritual movement, and draw about him a dozen companions, mostly fishermen along the coast, and suppose he should work with them for a year or two, and then ask them a question concerning his identity. Surely they would be surprised at his question, but still more surely it would never occur to any of them that this man was divine. If he began implying that he was, I feel certain they would try to get him into the hands of an alienist, and disperse the movement, and go back to their jobs. But that is not what happened here, in spite of their Jewish aversion to any man even remotely claiming divinity for himself. They all seem to have acquiesced in Peter's confession. And if they had not talked it over among themselves, and agreed upon it before, then Peter's flashing insight and faith so commended itself to them at that moment that they accepted it. You never hear of them dissenting subsequently from that belief, though it would have been the most easily disputed subject that could have arisen, and a dispute that would have broken His movement to pieces. Here is a perfectly amazing and unique thing. What do you make of it.?

St. Paul's Testimony

Soon after them arose another follower who never saw

Jesus in the flesh, but saw Him in His risen glory when He appeared to him one day while the man was on his way to destroy Christian belief so far as he could. And after Saul's conversion, when he became Paul, he believed without question that Jesus was God. He says it again and again in his letters. "In Him dwelleth all the fulness of the Godhead bodily," and "declared to be the Son of God with power," and "the image of the invisible God, the firstborn of all creation." Here was a very great intellect, going to work on what he had heard from others, and what he had experienced himself. What do you make of his conclusion?

What Jesus Thought of Himself

Still more inescapable than the opinions others held of Him is what Jesus evidently thought of Himself. If you think that Simon Peter may have been enthused at the moment when he made his great confession at Caesarea Philippi, surely you must know that Jesus would have cut him down promptly if He had not accepted Peter's confession. In fact He did cut him down about something else a very brief while after. But not about this. He said, "Blessed art thou, Simon, for flesh and blood hath not revealed it unto thee, but my Father which is in heaven" (Matthew 16:17). And He went on to say that He would found His Church on that confession of faith. I cannot imagine any other honest, decent religious man accepting any such allegation concerning himself; he would reject it summarily as blasphemy and reprimand the speaker. Not so Jesus. He evidently believed that it was the simple truth.

He said many other things about Himself that point to the same end. We hear the familiar words, "Come unto me, all ye that labour and are heavy laden, and I will give you rest" (Matthew 11:28). But what utter egotism and blasphemy to claim to be able to take the burdens from men and give them peace, unless He is able to do it, and unless He has an authority far beyond the power of ordinary men! "He that hath seen me hath seen the Father." You cannot say more than that, unless He went a little beyond it when He said, "Before Abraham was, I am." Here is a Galilean peasant who declares, "All power is given unto me in heaven and on earth" (Matthew 28:18). These are maniacal claims unless they are true. The unbridled egotism of them, if they can be untrue, rules Jesus out, not only as a Saviour and Guide, but even as a good man. What do you make of it?

I have thought long and often about these things. And I have concluded that there are three possible interpretations of Jesus' clear belief that He was the Son of God.

Was He Deceived?

(1) He may have been deceived about Himself. The sense of power may have grown on Him, until it overwhelmed Him, and He began having delusions of grandeur. I saw a man once in a state hospital for the insane who thought he was the messiah, dressed in white robes, grew a long brown beard and flowing hair, till he looked much like the Holman Hunt pictures of Jesus. But this theory causes a difficulty. We must admit that He saw the truth about life more steadily, more accurately, than any other that ever lived. Is it psychologically possible that a man deceived about himself could utter truths that have become humanity's norm for truth in the moral and spiritual realm? Personally I cannot believe it. The two things do not match.

Was He Deceiving?

(2) He may have been deliberately deceiving the men about Him. If they believed Him divine, He could do more with them; they would sacrifice more for Him. There have been others in history, and in contemporary life, who have

allowed the fantastic claims of followers that they were
divine to stand unopposed, for it makes the cult stronger.
But let us remember one thing: Jesus died largely because
He made Himself equal with God—and that was supreme
blasphemy for the Jews. If He were simply deceiving, do
you not think that when the nails began going through the
flesh of His hands, He would have said, "Let up. I did not
mean it that way"? Yet He did nothing of the sort. Again, I
cannot imagine anyone sacrificing for others what He sacri-
ficed, only to fool them in the end as to His own identity.
Every reasonable thing in me recoils from both these theories
as being as untenable as they are horrible.

Was He Speaking Truth?

(3) The third possible interpretation is that His belief
was true. He was the Son of God, God incarnate, God—made
man. For once in all time the immortal and invisible God
condescended to become mortal and visible, for the sake of
man and his redemption. Why did God thus "empty himself,"
as St. Paul teaches, and take the form of a man? It was for
us men and women and for our salvation. "God so loved
the world . . . " That is the reason. Years ago I stood
in the baptistry of the Church of St. John Lateran in
Rome. It is rather a small room, and on its ceiling are some
beautiful, ancient, dark mosaics. I stood straining up to see
them, when I felt something thrust into my hand. A guard
had given me a tiny mirror. And when I looked down into
the mirror, I saw perfectly reflected the mosaics which were
above my head and difficult for me to see. Something like
that Jesus has done for us with regard to God. In Him we
see the perfect reflection of God. God as He is. This is the
faith of the Church from the beginning, and of the Bible. A
few have dissented from it, but the vast majority have held
it. Dr. Latourette, in his great *History of the Expansion of*

Christianity, says "Types of Christianity which had failed to stress the centrality of Jesus as God's Christ had not shown the power to reproduce themselves many centuries . . . In the first century that had been an assertion of faith. By the twentieth century experience had made it demonstrated fact."

If it be true that Jesus is God come in the flesh, then some things follow.

The God-Made Man

1. There has been a conjoining of God and man such as was never even conceived of elsewhere. Many religions, Mohammedanism and some kinds of Christianity, have so emphasized the holiness and the "otherness" of God that all real connection between Him and man is virtually impossible. This disappears in the God-made Man. All other faiths, depending as they do upon what inspiration fallible men may gather and weave into a belief, are like stalagmites, reaching up from the ground towards heaven. But the Christian religion is like a stalactite, reaching down from heaven towards earth. One rises from the floor of things, the other depends from the ceiling. Now, as you have seen in caves, sometimes the two meet and join in a solid pillar. This just is what happened in Jesus. In His human nature He reaches right down to the floor where we live and are; in His divine nature He comes down from the top, and in Him the two columns join in such perfect junction that it is like smooth marble in a polished pillar. God and man are at one in Jesus, the God-made Man.

The "Way" Is Plain

2. If Jesus is God, His teachings are not human precepts but divine commands, and His spoken truths are not guesses but revelations, and we really do have something sure in this world upon which we can lay hold with our minds and with our lives. There is more knowledge and more access

to knowledge in our day than ever before, and there is more
uncertainty and inner insecurity. Human wisdom is not
enough. We need divine truth and revelation. Our univer-
sities and places of learning will prove to be blind guides
unless they lead these insecure, seeking young people, not
alone to knowledge and the beginnings of wisdom, but to
the Source of all wisdom. Educated men have almost destroyed our civilization, and can almost destroy the planet,
because they have not known that which needs to be known
most, and that is how to live, and how to live with others. If
Jesus be God, we are not in the dark about God, or about
God's basic will for man, or about the way we were meant
to live our lives today. The world's wise men are yet not
wise enough. We need truth direct from God, and in Jesus
we have it.

Make Up Your Mind!

3. Neutrality concerning Jesus is impossible. It Jesus be
the maniac or the impostor that He must be if His belief in
His divinity is untrue, then He is not a good man but a
very evil man, and His religion, far from being something
about which one may remain merely tolerant, is something
which one ought to fight as false and wrong. The Communists
would then be right, and our Christianity is opium. I can
understand anyone believing in Christ, or rejecting Him, but
l cannot understand anyone in the name of "reason" taking
the liberal attitude that Jesus is a very nice Man who was
so kind that He ought to be tolerated and even encouraged.
He wasn't that kind of person! Stop thinking He was! He
was quiet and patient in His Spirit, but He whipped traders
out of the temple, and He lashed the Pharisees with words
that burned and scorched, and He pressed His truth upon
men without compromise, and He made claims for Himself
which prove Him mad or prove Him God. Get over the

silly notion that Jesus was just a sweet person in a long white robe who patted children on the head and never offended anybody. He claimed to be God and He still claims it, and you cannot be neutral about Him. Kierkegaard was right, there are only two attitudes you can take toward Him, believe in and accept Him, or be offended in Him. You take Him or you reject Him. Many in our time, led by the blind leaders of the blind in some academic circles, make an intellectual smoke-screen of theoretical secularism and naturalism, which have in them no place for Jesus and His divine claims. Behind these intellectual theories I think some hide their own frank fear of coming out and exposing themselves to the light as it is in Christ and facing honestly His overwhelming claims. Did these men make the universe? Did they release the merciful forces that came from Christ and have increasingly made life tolerable and happy for those who come under Christ's influence these past nineteen centuries? Whom do they make themselves? If they would be indifferent to Christ and His claims, will they take the full consequences of their act, and face the indisputable fact that the diminishing influence of Jesus in history would mean the increasing defeat and downfall of man himself? The best in this world came from Jesus. His power over the lives of men is in no wise lessened from the first. We must fight Him, and take the consequences of being a traitor to our own race; or we must follow Him, and take the consequences of being in part responsible to bring the whole of mankind to Him in faith. This is the issue, because Jesus is God.

"I am trying to prevent anyone from saying the really silly thing that people often say about Him: 'I'm ready to accept Jesus as a great moral teacher, but I don't accept His claim to be God.' That's the one thing we mustn't say. A man who was merely a man and said the sort of things Jesus said wouldn't be a great moral teacher. He'd be either a lunatic—on a level with a man who says he's a poached egg—or else he'd be the Devil of hell. You must make your choice. Either this man was, and is, the Son of God, or else a madman or something worse. You can shut Him up for a fool, you can spit at Him and kill Him for a demon; or you can fall at His feet and call Him Lord and God. But don't let us come with any patronizing nonsense about His being a great human teacher. He hasn't left that open to us."

From
The Case For Christianity
By
C. S. Lewis

(From letter to the late Canon S. M. Shoemaker from the Rev. R. E. M.)

Glendale, Calif.
December, 1960

Dear Dr. Shoemaker:

May I again express my deep and heartfelt appreciation of your ministry through "This Week's Word"?

These sermons feed my soul and inspire my own sermons, as they have since I first heard you. I heard you first on the radio when I was a young pastor in the mountains of Pennsylvania and Virginia.

I remember the one which gave me clear intellectual faith in the divinity of Christ. I refer to this last one called, "Why I Believe That Jesus Is God," and it is more meaningful now than it was the first time I heard you give it on the radio, many years ago. I remember, too, how it helped the laymen in my congregation then, and now I shall use the sermon again out here in California.

Thank you for the clear way you bring to us the reasons

for our faith that God is indeed like His Son Who reflected God's love so perfectly in all Jesus said and did. The reasons for our faith are all there in what you say so well about Jesus.

May you live long to help ministers with their own faith and ministering.

Faithfully,
R. E. M.

(From letter to Mrs. C. C. O.)

Glendale, Calif.
February, 1964

Dear Mrs. O:

Just a few days before your letter came I had heard of Dr. Shoemaker's "graduation," as I like to think of his death. It was the sermon called, "Why I Believe That Jesus Is God" that I remember best, and used throughout my ministry.

I shall never forget his clear and convincing statement of the deity of Christ, and am sure that this one sermon, if there had been no others, would have spoken to ministers and laymen alike. Dr. Shoemaker's "T.W.W." spoke to people everywhere. It was an honor to know Dr. Shoemaker, even through his words. Thank you for giving me this opportunity to say how I benefited by 'T.W.W." I never met Dr. S., but I feel that I knew him well, through his books and his sermons.

I look forward to a collection of "T.W.W."

Gratefully,
R. E. M.

[The following exchange of letters referring to "People Under Conviction" is used with "Why I Believe That Jesus Is God," because it has been useful to a minister in bringing people to Christ; and this was Canon Shoemaker's main purpose in life.—C. O.]

(From letter addressed to "T.W.W.." after Canon Shoemaker retired)

Calvary Episcopal Church
Pittsburgh, Pennsylvania

Att: "This Week's Word"
Gentlemen:

Do you have on hand any unused copies of the sermon entitled, "People Under Conviction," released through T.W.W.? If so, I will be glad to have them as I have distributed this sermon to many people of my parish and those outside of it, who were counseling with me about their desire to find a close relationship to Christ. Sometimes these people under conviction of the need of Christ search for help, and this sermon of Dr. Shoemaker's contains unusual insights into the hearts and minds of persons who are beginning the search. I have used it also with the relatives of such persons, i.e. those who have already attained the surrender in *their* lives, and it has helped them to be more understanding of those who still are seeking.

For an example, there are two sisters in my parish who have both been life-long Episcopalians. The one who had already taken the step of surrender thought the behavior of her sister, who was only starting to feel conviction of her need, was bizarre. I gave her Dr. Shoemaker's "People Under Conviction" to read, after which she was able to work *with* the Holy Spirit, and to understand her sister who now has come to complete healing.

This explains my need of this one sermon. If you have no

copies left over, I will understand, of course.
    Thank you.

Gratefully,
Dean M. E. McT.

(From letter to Mrs. C. C. O. from Dean M. E. McT. after
    Canon Shoemaker died)

Sacramento, Calif.
March, 1964

Dear Mrs. O:

Thank you for writing me of the project you are working
on with Sam's sermons. His insights and courage in preaching them, came through all he said and was. I wrote after
he retired for additional copies of "People Under Conviction," which I have used over and over again.

I am happy that in February of 1963 I was able to visit
Dr. Sam in Pittsburgh for a brief period. Obviously, he was
not well then, but there was no dimming of his wonderful
spark and humor. After renewing old acquaintance, he and
I talked of the church.

"You know," he said with the characteristic chuckle, "I
think that putting a new convert into some churches is like
putting a new chick under a dead hen."

We will always miss him. God bless your efforts to spread
his evangelistic work.

Sincerely,
(Dean) M. E. McT.

CHAPTER 8

THE NATURE
OF CHRISTIAN LOVE

"St. Paul says that love is patient, and patience comes from a deep knowledge that none of us is in any position to be impatient with others; we are all in the same boat. Patient love is the quietness that believes that God will win out in the long run. Only faith can dare to be patient."

From
The Experiment of Faith
By
Samuel Moor Shoemaker

If we have ever seen a real Christian (and all of us have), we know that what impressed us most was not that he was loving. Somehow he had more patience with exasperating people, more hope about wicked people, more time for tedious people, and—most particularly—more forgiveness toward his opponents, than the rest of us have. Sometimes we write him off as having a more equable and easy disposition than we have or say he doesn't have to do with as vexing people as we do; but we just can't get away from the fact that there is a little register within us, even the most pagan of us, that knows when a person is being a Christian in his

life, and when he is not. And our gauge and standard is
largely what is best called by the name of love.

Love In The Gospel

This is true to the Gospel. There is a great deal about faith,
there is a great deal of simple and relevant theology, there is
a great deal of talk about money and truthfulness and God
and prayer and many other important things connected with
the Christian religion, in the Gospels. But when the scribe
asked Jesus which commandment was first, Jesus said, "You
shall love the Lord your God with all your heart, and with
all your soul, and with all your mind. This is the great and
first commandment. And a second is like it, You shall love
your neighbor as yourself. On these two commandments depend all the law and the prophets." (Matthew 22:37-40,
RSV. These are not terms of belief, nor of rectitude of outward conduct. They concern the feelings of the heart toward
God and toward people. And when it came to the Final
Judgment, Jesus did not say a word about what a man believed; but only about whether he had been loving: "Inas-
much as ye did it—or did it not—unto one of the least of
these my brethren, ye did it—or did it not—unto Me."

I think our best study of the nature of Christian love can
be made through watching Jesus, and seeing how He acted
in different situations. It is well enough to study St. Paul's
great chapter (I Corinthians 13), and hear his wonderful
analysis of the constituents of Christian love—such as patience, kindness, good manners, persistence—but let us see
what Jesus did.

Love Is Kindness

Take the story of the wedding in Cana. Jesus was there as
one of the guests, as were His disciples. Probably more people came than had sent their acceptances, and there was not

enough wine. The host was in a most embarrassing predicament. His mother told Jesus about it, and received what can only be taken as a rebuke from Him—possibly because He had already noticed the situation. There were six stone jars standing empty near by, and they were big ones, holding twenty or thirty gallons apiece. Jesus told the servants to fill them with water. Then He told the caterer to take some of the contents to the bridegroom. The caterer was evidently not aware that a miracle had taken place, and he said to the host that most people serve the best wine first, and when people have had enough, then the poorer kind; but he had kept the best till the last. This was a simple act of kindness. It was without stint. One hundred and twenty gallons of wine is a lot of wine. Jesus might have acted differently in a country and time like ours, when all alcoholic drinks are often taken in gulps, too much and too fast. This was evidently not a problem. Jesus helped the man fulfill his responsibilities as a host. It was a pure act of human kindness. That is love.

The other evening I was listening to some laboring men talking about what they were doing to make faith real and put it into action in the plants where they work. All of them emphasized how important was what they called ministry to those they wanted to interest in faith; i.e., visiting them when they were sick, thinking of their material needs, being concerned about their human interests. Christian love has time for simple human kindness.

Love Is Imagination

Take the story about Zacchaeus. It is to me one of the most human of all the stories of our Lord. He came into the city of Jericho. And Zacchaeus was short and couldn't see, and—like a boy watching a parade—he climbed up a sycamore tree. Jesus must have had some "pull" to him, and asked who he was. He was a tax collector and therefore despised and unpopular. He was short, and he was in an undignified position. But Jesus came up under the tree, called him by name, and told him to come down, for He would like to stay at his house. If we understand the custom of the time, this was conferring a kindness more than asking one. It must have been that, as they walked along, Jesus asked him about his work, and whether he liked it, and whether he liked himself for doing it. The crowd berated Jesus for going to the house of such a man. But the effect of Jesus' coming on Zacchaeus was that Zacchaeus said he was going to give half his money to the poor, and restore fourfold to anybody he had defrauded. And Jesus said, "Today salvation has come to this house. . . . The Son of man came to seek and save the lost." That was love.

See the quick flexibility in Jesus' mind, His imagination about what this man enjoyed in giving hospitality, the searching talk that must have come in somewhere for Zacchaeus to repent so handsomely. Quickly, by one imaginative gesture, a low-grade character was changed. Would you and I have seen the changed man in that little gnarled Jew up the tree? Would we have followed an impulse to ask a favor of him? Would we not have been balked by being his guest, from going right on to talk with him about his problem and his wrong? Love never damns people down into the categories they have fixed for themselves by past wrongs. This throws light on St. Paul's words, "Love believes all things, hopes all things. . . ." Have we love like that? Christian love is flexible, imaginative, redeeming by its own hopefulness, expecting great things of God and—yes—of human nature.

Love Is Honesty

Take the story of the rich young ruler. He must somewhere have heard Jesus speak, and he sought Him out and began at once on a high spiritual level, as though his interests were of the finest. "What must I do to inherit eternal life?" Jesus rehearsed the chief commandments. And the man said, "All these have I observed from my youth." It says that Jesus "looking upon him loved him." There must have been a winsome quality in his spiritual search, even if it was in the end sentimental and a little self-satisfied. And out of this same love, Jesus said to him, "You lack one thing; go, sell what you have, and give to the poor, and you will have treasure in heaven." At this his countenance fell, for he was very rich. He didn't own his possessions, they owned him. And so he went away "sorrowful"—sorrowful that the price was so high. We do not know what became of him—whether he thought it over and returned, or whether the price was always too high. This, too, was love, for Christ to tell him the truth.

Do we know that love just must often thwart another's ego? So many of us have contracted a modern habit of wanting to please everybody and get along with everybody. We like to call this love. But love without truth is sentimentality, as truth without love may be cruelty. One of the Proverbs says, "Faithful are the wounds of a friend" (27:6). I know of a woman who got into a terrible marriage because some of her friends who knew what kind of a man she was marrying would not "hurt her feelings" by telling her—so they let her find out by misery and suffering. That's not love—that's what the modern age calls "chicken." Love often tells unwelcome truth, as Jesus had to tell the rich young ruler.

Love Is Sacrifice

The Cross was love. And we must remember that it is one thing to do one sudden, impulsive, generous thing that costs very little and is soon behind us; it is another to take a line of living that you know is going to be for the larger good but will work against your own personal interests, or at least not forward them. The Cross began almost as soon as Jesus was born. There is that in human nature which crucifies what it admires but is challenged by it. Jesus' whole life was a judgment on the contemporary ecclesiastics, and they did not like Him. He was doing the thing they were talking about. He was releasing the power they thought they had locked up in their pious little routines and petty church ways. That steady course, that Face "set to go to Jerusalem" where the final act would be wrought out, that series of a thousand little crosses that did not add up to exemption from the big Cross, but instead brought it nearer all the time, there was a Cross that did not stand on a hill "without a city wall," but stood in a human heart throughout His whole life of service.

Love And Forgiveness

We must always believe that the very heart of the Cross is forgiveness. That's what the Cross was primarily about— God's forgiveness of man. How easy to approve of the idea, but to resist the actual transaction! For to be forgiven by God, we must first ask God to make us penitent, so that we are in some position to receive forgiveness. It is hard to be sorry for our sins—much easier to be brazen about them, or just try to forget them. Only the Spirit of God can put a genuine sense of repentance in our hearts, that will reflect our knowledge of how much our sins disappoint God, and how much they hurt other people, and what damage they do to our own immortal souls. At least we know enough of the nature of God to know that He wants us to repent and He wants us to be forgiven.

But all this has a corollary. "If you do not forgive men their trespasses, neither will your heavenly Father forgive you your trespasses." This is not a legalistic "quid pro quo": this is the affirmation of an eternal spiritual law. The forgiveness of God must complete a circuit through us to others whom we should forgive; and if we stop that flow of forgiveness anywhere, we stop it altogether. God cannot forgive us unless we are ready to forgive others.

I don't know where this finds you, but I know where it finds me. The other morning some of us were together in a church where the rector was saying Morning Prayer, and leading us in guided silent prayer. He said, "Let us pray for those whom we love." And that was easy. Then he said, "Let us pray for those whom we do not love." And there rose up before my mind three men for whom I had to pray. They were men who have opposed my work. In this they may have been wrong. But my wrong was in resentment and a feeling of letting myself be cut off from them, and even from praying for them, because of it. Years ago I read a quotation from Mary Lyon that recurs to me again and again: "Nine-tenths of our suffering is caused by others not thinking so much of us as we think they ought." If you want to know where pride nestles and festers in most of us, that is right where it is; and it is not the opposition of others, but our own pride, which causes us the deepest hurt. I suggest you get hold of that quotation and make it the basis of your Lenten self-examination. I never read a word that penetrated more deeply into the sin of pride from which all of us suffer, nor one which opens up more surgically our places of unforgiveness.

Love Is Of God

Whence shall we come by such love as we ought to have? How inexpressibly shallow it is for anyone to think he can achieve it in his own strength! We can rationalize and justify almost anything when we are away from God. It takes nothing less than His grace in full operation in our souls to make us ready or even able to see these deep things in our justification, which is almost the very opposite of love. It will take a revolution if we are to change in any deep and significant way. The war we deplore in the world begins first in our own hearts; and that is where peace must be born. Peace is not just a warm feeling of amiableness, its base is always forgiveness, beginning with asking for and accepting God's forgiveness of us. It is the nature of Christian love that first we allow ourselves to be loved by God, i.e. to become what He wants us to become.

Let us today open ourselves to Him in a deeper self-surrender which will accept His overwhelming love, and then manifest it in our daily walk with other people!

"In essential things, unity. In doubtful things, liberty. In all things, love." —Phillip Schaff

(From letter to Canon Shoemaker from the Rev. Tom Parker, head of Methodist Church of South Africa)

Cape Town, South Africa
January, 1960

Dear Dr. Shoemaker:

Thank you for all your guidance and inspiration, received through "This Week's Word." Every word you write means more to me than any other writer or speaker I know in my contemporary world. We in Africa pursue our witness for Christ, and this is truly a troubled land. I just wanted you to know that my own churches are seeing better light by following the pattern you set out for us from time to time.

Our prayer is that you may live long to continue your great work for our Lord and His Church in our time.

Your friend in Christ,
T. P.

(From letter from Canon Shoemaker to the Rev. Tom
   Parker)

Pittsburgh, Pa.
March, 1960

Dear Mr. Parker:

Your letter makes me feel very close to you, and you are
generous to say the things you say of "T.W.W." I am deeply
grateful that God has used these sermons where He is so
terribly needed as He is needed in Africa now.

One feels so sure about our Lord, and His Gospel, and so
un-sure about oneself, and the best way to bring the Gospel
to typical people in our time. A letter like yours is both
heartening and humbling.

God bless you deeply in your ministry. Maybe one of these
days we will have a chance to talk together face to face.
Meantime, it is good to be in touch through the printed word.

May God bless and use you,

Faithfully,
S. M. S.

(From letter to Mrs. C. C. O. from the Rev. Tom Parker)

Durban, South Africa
February, 1964

Dear Mrs. O:

I had not heard that Canon Shoemaker had died. He will
be greatly missed out here as we used his sermons called
"T.W.W.," and I still use them and remember one especially
which gave me unspeakable help in my own ministry. It was
called, "The Nature of Christian Love," and still to me is the
best and most useful sermon on this subject I have ever read.

Canon Shoemaker was a very great man, and to me he

was the John Wesley of the Christian Church in our time.
With my prayers for what you are doing,
Sincerely,
Tom Parker

(From letter to Mrs. C. C. O. from Mr. David Griffith)

Pittsburgh, Pa.
September, 1964

Dear Mrs. O:
I loved Sam as we all do because he loved us so much. The
first time I talked with him was at a Men's club meeting at
Calvary Church. After dinner it seemed natural to tell him
what was on my mind about the steel strike at the mills all
over the city. From that moment, I knew that he was concerned about me and what I was thinking, and also about
what God is thinking, and wants us to do. Sam asked me to
come to his study the next morning at eight o'clock, and I
was there.

We talked about the strike and all that it meant to me
and so many others. Then Sam said, "Well, let's pray about
this." I was to learn that Sam always prayed before he offered his own opinion. After we had prayed to know how
we could be used in this matter, Sam went back to his desk,
and I read. At ten-thirty we went across the street to a communion service, but before we went we agreed that each
would pray about the strike, and write down whatever
thoughts came to us then.

When we were back in Sam's study, we compared notes
and found that we had both written the very same thing,
that I should try to talk to the top man. We had a very short
prayer and I left, but that was the beginning of my love for
Sam. He made me see a self I did not know I had, as the

years passed, and while I did not ever get to the top man, the whole atmosphere began to change in the mill as I followed Sam's leading to bring more love to bear in our lives there, and faith in God, *Sam's* very practical God.

Soon the strike was ended, and Sam and I rejoiced.

Sam was really concerned about people, and he made me feel that he and our Lord understood what I felt, and what I was trying to say and do. He understood the simplicity of my faith, but most of all he really loved people, all sorts of people, and showed it in his genuine concern for whatever condition was theirs. Once he said to me, "Dave, if you have a hole in your shoe, my own foot is cold." That is Christian love.

In the fall of 1963 I was asked to come to York, Pennsylvania to help conduct a Retreat. I doubted if I could make it physically* to see Sam at "Burnside" although it is only fifty miles further. I did call him and decided to go to see him. It was the last time I saw Sam alive. I have talked with him on the phone many times since, and the last time he said to me, "Dave, we may not get to see each other again here, but I'll see you on the other side." He might have been saying, "I'll see you soon, in Pittsburgh."

And that is how I think it is with Sam. I know that he is alive, only now he is with our Lord and the others he wanted so much to know. I know this, absolutely, and believe that he is working overtime helping me and so many as he did when he was here. I believe that God's special assignment to Sam is what it was here, the assignment to love people and care about doing God's will always.

Sam is with me still, and I often feel him beside me when I am working late and am alone in the mill.

Thank you for letting me write this letter about our friend.

Lovingly,
Dave

Author's footnote to above letter: David Griffith is the young man to whom Canon Shoemaker referred in Chapter III of his book called, *The Power of God*, published by Harper & Row. It reads, "Not long after coming to Pittsburgh I gave a talk to a couple of hundred men in our Men's Club at Calvary Church. After the dinner a man of about thirty-five came to me. He turned out to be one David Griffith, a steel worker in the Homestead plant of the United States Steel Company, a member of the C.I.O. union. I had no idea how much leadership was in this quiet fellow who wanted to settle the steel strike then, through more Christian relationships."

*Footnote to Dave's reference to his trip to York, Pennsylvania and his physical condition: Mr. Griffith is a victim of advancing multiple sclerosis. In spite of this, his faith is tried, but not diminished. He is still a radiant Christian, as "clear as sunlight through a clean window," as "Dr. Sam" once said of David Griffith.

CHAPTER 9

WHAT DOES "THE ATONEMENT" MEAN

When Jesus came to Golgotha they hanged Him on a tree,
They drove nails through hands and feet and made a Calvary.
They crowned Him with a crown of thorns, red were His wounds and deep,
For those were crude and cruel days, and human flesh was cheap.
When Jesus came to Birmingham they simply passed Him by,
They never hurt a hair of Him, they only let Him die.
For man had grown more tender, and they would not give Him pain,
They only just passed down the street, and left Him in the rain.
Still Jesus cried, 'Forgive them for they know not what they do,'
And still it rained the winter rain that drenched Him through and through.
The crowds went home and left the streets without a soul to see,
And Jesus crouched against a wall, and cried for Calvary.

G. Studdert-Kennedy

99

"But God shows his love for us in that while we were yet sinners Christ died for us." Romans 5:8, RSV.

What has the death of Jesus Christ on the cross to do with your and my redemption? We stand in awe of a Man ready to give His life for His cause, and we feel unique awe when this Man is such a man as Jesus Christ. But how can someone's death on a cross in Palestine more than nineteen centuries ago have anything to do with my eternal status before God? St. Paul clearly says, and the Nicene Creèd takes it up so that we repeat it every time we make that great declaration of faith, that "Christ died for us." What can it really mean?

Before we go into this, we must try to understand the problem with which the Atonement deals. We find a reflection of it, I think, in our dealings with our children, and with all who make mistakes and do wrong, in which company, of course, we belong ourselves. The wrongdoing creates an estrangement from those who seem to stand for the right. The child fears to tell the father what he really did; or the person who has done a wrong wants to keep out of the way of anyone who knows it. There ought to exist in the heart of that father a pure and redemptive love towards that child, or in the heart of someone offended towards the offender.

But we must remember the holiness of God as well as the love of God. In this case we are not dealing with two fallible human beings who have somewhere done a wrong, but with sinful men in relation to a perfectly holy God. What we know of His nature, and especially the revelation of Him that comes through the Cross, makes us aware of His love. What is going to impress upon us with equal force God's righteousness, God's holiness, and His demand of holiness upon ourselves?

Again, we catch reflections of this on the human level,

especially when someone is willing to go the length of real self-sacrifice and suffering in order to move the conscience of an offender as to the real seriousness of his offense.

In Dan Crawford's *Thinking Black,* he tells the story of a queen of one of the African tribes who became a Christian, though her husband did not. When the king died the tribe prepared to carry out an ancient custom of burying six beautiful maidens alive with him that they might wait on him in the other world. The queen, now a Christian, was horrified at this, and as a substitute offered herself, saying, "My royal blood is equal to the blood of these six maidens and I will substitute myself for them." This deed of complete sacrifice shocked the whole tribe, so that they put away the barbarous practice.

Ignatius Loyola knew a man who was engaged in an illicit love affair. Nothing would move him to repentance concerning it. There ought to be a readiness to forgive, and even a readiness to help the offending person find a mind of repentance so that forgiveness is possible.

But this does not mean that the readiness to forgive is all that is necessary. There is the matter of right and wrong— not only of a personal wrong to be righted if possible by restitution and amendment, but of a general wrong towards the moral law. With all our desire to make a child, or an offender, feel our love and concern, we must help them feel the essential wrong in the thing that has been done. This must be done in love, not in anger nor reprisal of any sort. But we must not let people get away with wrongdoing. This is not love, but sentimentality. There is law to be remembered as well as love. There is something more than their personal relationship to us that is at stake.

Now this is really a very pale reflection of the situation between man and God. The actual condition of our souls, once we are awakened, is just this: we are estranged from God, we are homesick for Him, and we cannot get back to Him by ourselves. Insofar as we seem to be able to span the chasm by ourselves, we are being proud and making it wider. Insofar as we merely accept the chasm, becoming more and more conscious of it, we decline into despair and perhaps a denial of our organic relation to God altogether. God's mind toward us is always and at all times a mind and will of love. Any belief about life, and any theory of Atonement that denies or forgets this is untrue.

The woman involved lived in the suburbs of the city, and the road to her house led across a bridge. Ignatius waited for the man, and when he came Ignatius plunged into the freezing water of the stream, and called out as the man crossed the bridge, "Go on, wretched one, go on to your disgusting pleasures. Do you not see ruin hanging over your head? Are you not horrified by the curse that is close upon you? Here I will afflict myself for you until the just anger of God appears to be turned aside." The man was alarmed and struck by such an extreme proof of charity. He stopped, turned back, and broke off the relationship. Notice again the use of the word "for"—"for you." There seems no relation whatever to Ignatius, shivering in the stream, and the man's unlawful love affair. The connection lies, of course, in the vividness of the enacted sacrifice to gain the man's attention, in the concern which manifests, in the effectiveness of what was done to deter the man from his wrong.

My beloved old friend, Canon Warner, of London, Ontario, was a great redeemer of people. The worse they were, the better he loved them. He always went for the people in the greatest need. There was an alcoholic that he had counselled with many times, and he had gone to AA, but it always ended up in his rejecting help and going on a spree. One night he came in again after being terribly drunk. Canon Warner put forth no arguments. He put his head down in his hands on his desk and cried. The man said to him he did not know there was anybody who cared that much, gave his own life to Christ, and was cured.

I was working with another alcoholic who was a prodigal in about every possible sense. He had done everything that could be done to defame a good name and break the hearts of the people who loved him. He had a mother who was by no means sentimental about him, knew fully his faults, realized that bailing him out of scrapes and setting him up again was not the full answer, and wept her heart out for him many, many times. But she kept a wonderful balance between realism and redemptiveness. Nothing he could do would ever cause her to speak of the shame it has brought on her and the family, or to un-son him, or to withdraw her love from him. Her life for years was one long cross of atonement for him. And finally he was changed. It makes one think of the incident about Monica, the mother of St. Augustine, who went to a priest and begged him to reclaim her son. He said to her, "Go thy ways, and God bless thee, for it is not possible that the son of these tears should perish."

You see, nothing makes it so clear that you care for the person, and care for the moral law, like being willing to take on whatever sacrifice or suffering seems essential in the situation, or can be made germane to it. No declamation about sin and righteousness will do it. Besides, who is fit to make such a declamation anyway, as if they were somehow above this sinning person? Advice and moral badgering accomplish appallingly little. They may only drive the person farther into wrong. But the caring of the heart, and the readiness to sacrifice for him—even to suffering—that is another matter. the love and the law both "come through" this kind of act and attitude.

Now lift up, if you can, this human situation to the divine-human situation. As we have said, we have to do here with

Perfect Love and Holiness on the one side, and ourselves on the other. We cannot try to span the chasm ourselves without pride that soon widens it, or despair which begins to deny it. There is quite literally nothing we can do about it; our repentance is not anywhere near enough. God must Himself step into the breach. He must get man's attention by a dramatic act that shows both His Love and His Holiness. He must take on human sin—all of it—all of it all the way back to the beginning of man, and all the way forward to the end of time. There must be an act which reflects God's horror at our sin, and yet His complete identification of Himself with us even when we are in sin. Here is the mystery and magic of the Cross. "God shows His love for us in that while we were yet sinners Christ died for us." There you have the whole truth of the Atonement. We cannot understand pure Holiness, and there will ever be great mystery about God's love satisfying God's holiness on the Cross. But we can make a beginning at least of understanding it.

Some things must follow.

The first is that this comes nearer explaining everything than any other happening in the world. The riddle of the world and life is not solved by the Incarnation alone, nor by the Resurrection alone; the Cross and the Atonement pierce through more deeply to the tragedy and anomaly of life than anything else. God cannot get to us unless He comes right down into the middle of our sins and their effects, letting them disappoint and hurt Him, but not contaminate nor infect Him. He deliberately "became sin for us," in that completely identified sense, so that from within this complete oneness with us in our need and shame He might lift us up to our redemption and glory. Dr. Reinhold Niebuhr says, ". . . a suffering divine love is the final coherence of life."

The second is that we fully accept this faith in our hearts. This is belief in the redeeming efficacy of Jesus' death on the

Cross for man's sins. Do not confuse this with the "spirit" of the Cross. Deeds of kindness and good will, even of self-sacrifice, are good but they are not the same as understanding the Atonement, and putting one's faith in the Redeemer on His Cross. This may be much farther than you have yet seen in your faith. Do not stop till it carries you all the way through the Cross, else all you have is a barren ethicalism of good works and no redemption at all.

The third is that, if we know something of what it has cost God to get us redeemed, we shall try ever to walk in grateful imitation of His love, His holiness and His humility. We shall know that life is not good because it is pleasant and comfortable or fits our terms; life is good when we let God have charge of it, redeem it, guide it, use it for His purposes, and bring glory out of suffering and obedience. We shall love, suffer and hope—we shall not resist, fume and despair. We shall not live heedless of the moral law, like the libertines; nor forget the principles of redemptive love, like the moralists. We shall seek to please God and persuade others so; and we shall seek to redeem, and not hound, wrongdoers. Most of us are easygoing as regards ourselves, and judging as regards others. Let us rather judge ourselves, and be understanding and redeeming towards others.

For the Cross should produce in us, not alone an understanding of the great sacrifice of God for us on Calvary, and not alone a spirit of good will and services for others, but a continuous attitude of surprised and abashed thankfulness for all God's mercy to us in Christ, which manifests itself in lives which so carry their own crosses, and help others to do it, that we are always and at all times footnotes to the Great Cross where God, in lonely majesty, wrought out our salvation.

CHRISTUS REX

But now beneath the scepter in His hand
I see the mark of nails made there of old;
And still a scar got in an ancient land,
Scarce hidden by that crown of glorious gold.

That was a dream . . . I see Him truly now
No armored Christ, but Christ upon His knees
Who prays for us, with blood upon His brow
A lonely Man beneath the garden trees.

From
So I Stand By The Door and Other Poems
By
Samuel Moor Shoemaker

ATONEMENT

. . . And there was colloquy again in heaven.
There had been colloquy before.
And They had been there together,
The Spirit, and the Son, and the Most High.
They were exercised in mind,
For mankind was rebellious, and Evil was rampant,
And none considered God . . .
When upon their colloquy a prayer broke in,
The prayer of the prophet.
When They said, "Who will go for us?"
The prophet answered, "Here am I: send me."
And They sent him. And beyond all others
Up until that time, the prophet truly revealed God.
But the prophet was not God.

And there was colloquy again.
And this time it was the Son Himself that volunteered:

And the Others sent him.
He came down to earth through the body of a Woman,
And He lived the life of mortal man,
And He died such a death as no mortal man could die,
For besides being mortal man, He was also God Himself,
God in the flesh, God dying for the sins of man.
And He suffered and was buried,
And the third day He rose again.
And long, long after
There was colloquy again in heaven.
A man had died whom nobody really knew but They.
He had come up to the gates and cried for admission.

He had lived a fearsome life, defied God, ignored man,
Broken all the moral laws. Yet he asked admission,
Saying that at the very last he had repented and believed.
The Most High consulted with the Son and Spirit,
And He said, "What shall we do? For the man
Has broken every law. O that we could welcome him!
And yet thus to allow one who has disregarded all
    righteousness
To come within these gates is to risk
The integrity of the universe itself.
I bear up the pillars of it—they must not shake.
And what shall We do?"

There was no one else there but They three,
The Son, the Spirit and the Most High.
And the Spirit said, "He tried to repent at the end,
But he was too far gone by then to do more than mutter
A few words of regret and sorrow."
Then turning to the Son, the Most High said,
"What think You?"
And the Son, bearing still in His heart all the sins
Of all mankind forever, looked down, as if overwhelmed

With all the brood His death had brought streaming
Up to the Gates of Heaven—
The weak and the intemperate and the backsliders,
The sinners who hadn't known they were sinners,
The religious who found out at the last minute
That they had never been religious at all in their hearts,
And the indifferent who never realized till they were dying
That they must confront God, and called out to Christ,
And others who wrecked their lives,
And some who had helped to wreck the world,
And some with souls so shriveled and starved
That you would hardly call them souls at all—
As if these were too many, and too bad,
To bring before the Most High,
Who had in His custody the moral law of the universe,
And could not easily abate its high requirements . . .
And this last one seemed almost too much,
With his impudent defiance and nothing
But a wisp of aspiration for a soul . . .
The Son kept His face downwards,
And looked at His hands, almost like an awkward
Little boy, pleading mercy for a play-mate . . .
He just kept looking down
At His hands . . .
Till the Most High turned to see what He was doing,
And He caught sight of those Hands . . .
And then He turned and called, till all Heaven
Reverberated with the sound of His command,
"Let the man come in."

From
So I Stand By The Door and Other Poems
By
Samuel Moor Shoemaker

"An offender must be punished; I don't argue with that. But to punish and not to restore, that is the greatest of all offences. If a man takes upon himself God's right to punish, then he must also take upon himself God's promise to restore. There is a hard law—that when deep injury is done to us, we never recover until we forgive."

From
Too Late the Phalarope
By
Alan Paton

CHAPTER 10

LORD, TEACH US TO PRAY

"The answer to the problem of prayer seems to me to be answered in this principle, 'If any man willeth to do His will, he shall know how to pray, what to pray for, the power of prayer, the comfort of prayer. If any man willeth to do God's will, he shall know . . .' "

From
Obedience as a Condition of Knowledge
By
Samuel Moor Shoemaker

We all know in our experience, I think, that whatever the outward form or association of our religion, it is really alive and at work when we pray. It is a question whether merely following some ethical standard is in any true sense what Jesus Christ came to teach us. We must feel the reality of the Power behind all things—God—and be in touch with Him, and include Him in all our activities. We must know something of His direct influence over us, controlling, guiding, forgiving, caring for us. Religion is relationship with God; and, as much of relationship is talk and communication, prayer is the communion between God and ourselves.

What KIND Of God?

Whether anything happens in prayer depends on what kind of God God is. If He created the universe, and gave everything a primeval push, and then retired beyond where we can get in contact with Him, prayer is a vain effort. But if He be "the God and Father of our Lord Jesus Christ," He is not like that. He is concerned for the creation He made, and concerned with the people in it who are meant in fact to be His children. Most people in our day believe in some kind of God. There are very few atheists. Someone said an atheist is just a theologian with the jitters. But there are many who think God so great and so impersonal that He cannot possibly mean anything personal to us, and we cannot even say that He is a "personal" God.

Let me try to answer that, not from my own wisdom, but from that of the man who graduated at Princeton with the highest honors in all its history—"summa cum laude"—the late Dr. Henry Norris Russell, of the Department of Astronomy. One evening he had been giving us some head-splitting figures on the size of the universe. Talking with him afterwards, I said, "Dr. Russell, how is it possible that an infinite God can have time for us?" He replied (and I recall his exact words), "The trouble is that your infinite God is not infinite enough. If He is really infinite, He can dispatch the affairs of this universe in the twinkling of an eye, and then have all the time in the world for you." I have never forgotten it. He was a great scientist and a great Christian. His word gave great lift to a young man seeking foundations for his faith!

What KIND Of Prayer?

Prayer not only depends on what kind of a God God is; it depends upon the pray-er, and the kind of prayer that is offered. A while ago I was called to talk with a late teen-ager in the hospital. She said to me, "I've been kind of sore with God lately." I said, "Why?" She said, "I have asked Him to do a lot of things, and He hasn't answered my prayers." Well, I suggested we think about this a little. A person who has been ignoring God for a long time gets in some kind of a jam; and then all of a sudden rushes to Him with some telegraphic orders about what He should do. What kind of chaos would result if God tried to answer all the little selfish prayers of all the little selfish people in the world? The deep question is, Is God our celestial office boy, or are we His earthly servants? Is prayer a means of getting God to change His mind in our behalf, or is prayer seeking to find His mind and will? Our small children ask us for unreasonable and selfish things, and sometimes we give them to them because there seems to be no other way to express our love for them. God seems to me to do the same thing. But as there comes a day when you can reason with a child about what to do about a request, so God looks for the day when He can reason with us. The childish "gimme-gimme" prayer begins to give way to the more mature prayer of, "Lord, what do You want me to do? What is Your will in this situation?"

Prayer And The Rest Of Life

This means we cannot separate prayer from the rest of life. Many of us do what that girl did: we live our lives as we please, and then when things get into a snarl, we ask God to get us out of it. Soon or late we must face the implications of prayer. And they are principally that we become more and more the kind of people who pray because we love God and His will. Prayer is not calling in the fire department; prayer is seeking to live so that the house does not get on fire. Prayer is not the "last resort," it is the first thought in every situation—or at least the second. Either we shall bring the rest of life more in line with God's whole will and plan, or else prayer will be like nothing so much as the crying of a spoiled child. In the last analysis, prayer implies conversion. For conversion is the decision to turn our wills over to the will of God; and unless this has been done once in a decisive way, we shall not repeat it again and again in prayer, which is just wherein prayer should primarily consist. Prayer is communion between two people that increasingly know each other. And one of these "people" is very decidedly a Senior Partner in the relationship. Do any of you check in at the office in the morning to see what the boss wants you to do that day? I think that is very nearly what our morning prayer ought to be.

We're Always Praying!

Some weeks ago Bishop Pardue was having a Quiet Day for his clergy; and he quoted at second hand from Emerson a threefold idea about prayer. The first is that we are praying at all times, we are never not praying; "prayer is the soul's sincere desire," and what we keep desiring with all our hearts is what we really pray for. Second, prayers are being answered all the time. What we long for without cessation increasingly becomes a fact. Strong desire draws out of life what it wants and thinks it needs. Third, we must therefore be careful what our true prayer is, the real desire of the soul. Our deepest motivation is our prayer. This is why the service of Holy Communion begins with a prayer to a God "unto whom all hearts are open, all desires known." This is why merely saying words is not praying, but deep desiring— maybe as we walk along the street intensifying our determination about something we want to do or to get—is our real prayer. Right in the midst of the most selfish prayer in the world, we may catch ourselves and ask God to forgive the wrong of it and lift it to something better. We can pray to pray in the right way.

For What Shall We Pray?

Speaking of that, people are often in a quandary about how to pray in certain complex situations. A child is born that appears to be defective. Shall one pray for healing? Certainly—that seems best of all if it be in God's greater plan. If there should not be healing, should the child be taken home when one considers the effect upon other little children there; or should the child be placed where it can receive expert care? The most pressing thing is the anguish of the parents, asking how to pray right. Surely one is meant to pray for the healing; and for guidance in the right care of the child, should the full healing not be granted; and for grace to accept all this in such a way that real good comes out of real tragedy. Inevitably the question arises whether this was "God's will." One recoils from this. How can God will a defective child? It looks more as if something had slipped in nature. But we must not say that God has nothing to do with such a situation. He can give comfort and strength to anguished people, a peace deeper than pain, a strength greater than shock. He will guide as to right decisions. He will help to bear what must be, intellectually considered, a mystery. One does not bring to such a situation a dumb and enforced resignation, but a desire to surrender the situation in all its mystery and tragedy to God, asking what His will is now, in and for the situation. The capacity to bear something that cannot be understood is one of the gifts God alone can give to us. Let us not so much look for the perfect attitude in such a situation, or even to say the perfect words. Let us pour out the anguish we feel, ask for strength and guidance, and leave it to God how He ministers to us.

Pray About Everything

Some people have a strange idea that it is right to pray

about "spiritual" matters, and wrong to pray about "natural" or "secular" matters. They think it's right to pray for more faith, or even more health, but never for more income even when they need it. Do you think all God is interested in is the Sunday "you," but not the Monday-to-Friday "you?" Do you think He is only interested in the money you put in the plate, but not the money you put in your pocket or your bank account? I cannot find any real dividing line between the spiritual and the natural, the sacred and the secular. It seems to me that all of life is sacred in which God is included, and all life is secular from which He is excluded. Your job is as sacred as mine, if we both try to do them for God and with His help. Pray about whatever interests you. Pray about those things that threaten God as His rivals in your life—things like success and power. It isn't religion that interests God, I think, but life—all of it. He may change our present attitudes towards these natural interests, but I think whatever interests us interests Him. Dr. John W. Suter says, "What we ought to be praying about on Sundays are the things that keep us awake nights between Sundays."

Prayer and "Success"

Nothing that concerns prayer is more important than getting straight on the matter of prayer and prospering events. I still hear many people, who ought by now to know better, say things like this: "Why did this terrible thing happen to her? She is such a wonderful Christian." Have you never considered the Cross of Christ? That happened to the Best this world ever saw when He was thirty-three and at the height of His usefulness and power. Christ on a Cross—and you asking why something dreadful should come to you or someone else that is trying to live a good life? There is no guarantee in Christianity against trouble; there is guarantee against defeat. But we must consider all this in connection with something St. Paul said, "All things work together for good to them that love God" (Romans 8:28). When you have begun to put your trust in God, and turned your life and situation over to Him as fully as you can, and prayed about everything, and stopped trying to manage it yourself, you will discover just that—"all things work together for good." God takes some things out of our hands, and handles them better than we can. This concerns the ultimate best, not the immediate wish always. It will take faith to see and feel it sometimes. Everything depends on the depth of our commitment to God. It would not be true to say that when you pray you get everything you ask for; but it would be true to say that the more you pray, the better things go. God keeps you from self-centered worry, from licking the wounds of disappointment, from seeing life only as it converges on yourself.

This means that prayer is effective, not when we can point to this or that answer, but when the whole of life is more and more caught up on the fulness of God's will for us. Effective prayer is not measured by how much we manage to get out of God, but by how much of God we manage to let into daily living. Heightened energy, deepened faith, greater health of body and spirit, the conquest of moods, power to forgive people and accept their forgiveness of us—these are the things that result from prayer—not just getting what we think we need.

I do not believe that prayer ever changes God or His will of love; it cannot make Him more concerned than He was already without our prayers. It is not giving Him a new idea. Prayer links us up to God and may link others. Prayer may affect events. I believe it does; but it adds nothing whatever to God's wisdom and benevolence. It only makes us more receptive to the things He wants to give us. And the great shift-over from immature to mature prayer concerns the in-

creasing desire to want what He wants, rather than to demand what we want.

The Pattern Attitude In Prayer

This brings us to what should be the pattern prayer of all
our praying—not as touching the words we use—the Lord's
Prayer must forever be this—but as touching the deep attitudes out of which we pray. And this recalls Jesus' prayer in
Gethsemane, as found in Mark 14, verse 36: "Father, all
things are possible to thee; remove this cup from me; yet not
what I will but what thou wilt." There may, I believe, have
been considerable spaces between those three brief words.
The first is an affirmation: "Father, all things are possible to
thee." We affirm God's full power over all life, all events.
We say there is nothing that might not happen—we are in
the hands of a good and powerful God. That puts prayer in
its setting. Then comes the heart of the natural desire: "Remove this cup from me." He must have hated death, it was
so inappropriate for Him. Life was His word. He recoiled
from it. And He prayed honestly for what He desired, even
if He knew it was not the final stage of his prayer. We must
do the same: it is a form of honesty with God. And then
comes the purified prayer, "Yet not what I will but what
thou wilt." Death was not so bad as missing God's full purpose for Him which might only be fulfilled through the
Cross. That was what He really wanted and really prayed
for. It must be so with us. With whatever struggle (and we
cannot but think it was a superhuman struggle for Him to
turn from "remove this cup" to "yet not what I will but what
thou wilt") it is this which brings us to the place of power
in prayer. This does not mean sad resignation; this means
willing and glad cooperation. This means prayer that may
carry us to our own Calvary, but it means prayer with Resur-

rection wrapped in the dark folds of its struggle and mystery. Lord, teach us to pray as You prayed in Gethsemane!

"The proper outline of a Christian prayer is not, 'Please do for me what I want.' It is, 'Please do with me what You want!' That prayer will always be answered in proportion to its sincerity."
From
Bishop Richard S. M. Emrich's
Five Marks of a Healthy Parish
By
The Most Reverend William Temple
Archbishop of Canterbury

(From letter to Canon Shoemaker from G.F.)

California
August, 1959
Dear Dr. Shoemaker:

Someone gave me a copy of your sermon from "T.W.W." called, "Lord Teach Us To Pray," and it has helped me so much in my effort to accept Christ that I want a copy of my own. I am only 23 years old and have been an alcoholic for years, and can't gain freedom from drink by myself. I do not belong to your faith, but I need to learn how to pray, and this sermon means so much that I want a copy of my own. Please send me a copy of this sermon, and will you put my name on the mailing list for "T.W.W." as my friend who gave me this sermon tells me that you will send "T.W.W." to anyone who asks for it.

Thank you, and please pray that I may have the strength I need from God. I can't do this alone, as I have tried and failed many times.

Sincerely,
G. F.

(From letter to Mrs. C.C.O. from the Rev. F.E.V., Jr.)

Beverly Farms, Mass.

September, 1964

Dear Mrs. O:

As you may know from our friend, K. W., I am only one of thousands of men who first knew Sam on a college campus. As he puts it in the poem he wrote, "Apologia for my Life," 'the most important thing in the world is for men to find the door to God.'

Sam did just this for me on the Yale campus at a conference when I was there, and he did it more with his own contagious faith and his awareness of God in his own experience, his evident companionship with Christ, than by the things he said, great as those were.

Sam had a real ministry to college students, and I felt this through personal acquaintance with him, through time he spent with me, as also later at various times in New York.

To me, the most convincing effect of Sam's influence for Christ was the fact that on every campus he went to there developed interest in small prayer groups among the men and women. The prayer group became Sam's mark, and this approach to faith was exciting and creative, and caught on, whereas the conventional approach to religion we had known before, had not. Sam's demand for total commitment appealed to the idealism of youth, and the fact that Sam himself was joyous and that his joy was good-humored, all this undercut any hint of the preachy moralism which youth is rebelling against in our day.

The group I remember at Yale met weekly for worship and study, and it became of crucial importance to many of us. There we discovered for ourselves that the Christian faith is more than a rationalistic structure, but instead, the vessel of the living Spirit of God.

As do many other young men of our times, I trace my decision to enter the ministry to this deepening experience in the Prayer Group which Sam inspired at Yale. The experience of that prayer group gave me a faith which was and is adequate even for such a time as our own.

Prayer was the breath of Sam's faith, and in the sermon, "Lord, Teach Us To Pray," one of the F.A.W. series, Sam continued his prayer ministry, which I am sure will be felt for generations.

I am one among thousands who will be eternally grateful that Sam Shoemaker's shadow fell across my path.

Ministers all over the United States will never forget Sam, and will be interested in anything written about him now. Of this I am very sure.

Thank you for telling me of the collection, and I look forward to it.

Sincerely,
F. E. V., Jr.

PART THREE

WHAT THE HOLY SPIRIT CAN DO

CHAPTER 11

THE WORK OF THE HOLY SPIRIT

"There is a pneumatic quality of life when we come into the realm of Spirit-filled living that is very different from boot-strap religion."
From
God's Answer to Our Time
By
Samuel Moor Shoemaker

"And I will pray the Father, and he shall give you another Comforter, that he may abide with you forever; Even the Spirit of truth; whom the world cannot receive, because it seeth him not, neither knoweth him: but ye know him; for he dwelleth with you, and shall be in you."
John 14:16, 17

Pentecost Sunday is the great day of the gift of the Holy Spirit to the Church. We read the story in the second chapter of Acts. This was a corporate experience of the Holy Spirit: it was experienced together. The Holy Spirit was also given corporately to the Church at other times than Pentecost. Before our Lord's departure, He appeared to His disciples and breathed on them saying, "Receive ye the Holy Ghost. . . ." In Acts 10 there is an account of St. Peter preach-

ing, when "the Holy Ghost fell on all which heard the word."
The church came to associate the coming of the Holy Spirit
with the rite of apostolic prayer and the laying on of hands,
which we call Confirmation.

But for many of us these things sound remote and
strange. We find it hard to understand what happened at
Pentecost, because the Holy Spirit is Himself little known
to us. When St. Paul asked the Ephesians whether they had
"received the Holy Ghost since they believed," they said to
him, "We have not so much as heard whether there be any
Holy Ghost." And, except that most of us at least know His
Name, those words might carry an honest confession from
many even within the Church today.

There are eight names by which we can remember His
work and His function.

1. *The Holy Spirit is the Reflector.* "When the Comforter
is come, whom I will send unto you from the Father, even
the Spirit of truth, which proceedeth from the Father, he
will testify of me" (John 15:26). And again, "He shall not
speak from himself but what things soever he shall hear,
those shall he speak. ... . He shall glorify me, for he shall
take of mine, and shall declare it unto you" (John 16:13, 14).
The Holy Spirit is the Reflector of God the Father and of
Christ the Son. I want you to see in that the *oneness with the
Father and the Son,* which makes the Holy Trinity, one sub-
stance and three Persons; as we say in the Special Preface for
Trinity Sunday, "For that which we believe of thy glory, O
Father, the same we believe of the Son, and of the Holy
Ghost, without any difference of inequality." This oneness is
so complete that there can be difference of statement with-
out difference in truth: Christ says in one place of the Holy
Spirit, "Whom I will send you from the Father;" in another,
"Whom the Father will send you in my name." That is the
first great truth: His oneness with Father and Son.

The next great truth about the Holy Spirit as Reflector is His passive dependence upon the Father and the Son. "He shall not speak from himself, but what things soever he shall hear, these shall he speak" (John 16: 13). The Holy Spirit Who is the Guide of us all is Himself guided. And He speaks only as He is guided. All through this is seen the sovereign primariness of God the Father Almighty. But equally is the Holy Spirit the Reflector of Christ the Son: "He shall glorify me, for he shall take of mine, and shall declare it unto you." Will you take that truth quite simply, as I am sure it is meant? The Holy Spirit will emphasize just the things that Christ emphasized. The things He says to us will have been passed through Christ first, tested by Him, His guidance to us will always be in the spirit of Christ. And He will help us to understand and interpret Christ, help us to understand and interpret the things we read in the New Testament about Christ. He is in every sense the Reflector of the Father and of Christ.

2. *The Holy Spirit is the Reprover.* "And when he is come, he will reprove the world of sin, and of righteousness, and of judgment: of sin, because they believe not in me; of righteousness, because I go to my Father, and ye see me no more; of judgment, because the prince of the world is judged." The meaning of those concentrated words seems to be that Christ's own fate would raise the questions, "On whose side was the sin, and on whose side was the righteousness?" So a judgment would be involved. The Spirit would convict men of sin because they would find the error lay with those who rejected God's Messenger; the righteousness because the Spirit would show them that Christ's death was not the just punishment of a malefactor, but the manifestation of perfect righteousness which God accepted by taking Him to Himself; of judgment because the Spirit would show in time that the verdict which the power of this world had

passed against Christ was in reality the condemnation of
those who passed it (A. E. Brooke).

The reproving, convicting work of the Holy Spirit was not
confined to that early time; it is part of His everlasting
work. Do you understand what His conviction of us means?
Do you think that He goes about ferreting out all the wrong
He can find, and charging it up to us? This would be no
employment for a Spirit that is one with the God of love.
No, conviction is a form of enlightenment. Conviction is the
place where God says we need to be different, to act. Conviction is what keeps us from saying that the universe is
wrong, life is wrong, others are wrong, and makes us face
first of all the wrong in ourselves. I can do nothing about all
the wrong in the world until I have an answer for the wrong
in me; but I can have no answer until I admit the wrong
first, and I only admit it when I am willing to be convinced
or convicted of it. For most of us this is His beginning-work,
the place where He gives us a new beginning, a new start, a
fresh spiritual grasp and grip. He is the Reprover of human
sin.

3. *The Holy Spirit is the Regenerator.* "Except a man be
born of water and of the Spirit, he cannot enter into the
Kingdom of God." It would be a merciless thing if the all-
seeing Spirit of God should bring conviction to men, and
then there were no new life to give in place of the old. But
there is a new life. It is so new that Christ called it being
born over again. "That which is born of the flesh is flesh, and
that which is born of the Spirit is spirit" (John 3:5). The
Holy Spirit moves into the human life of a man or woman
and gives a new and supernatural life. This is not a man
seeing a high moral code and pledging himself to come up to
it: that is always doomed to some kind of disaster; for if he
measurably reaches it he becomes proud of his spiritual success; and insofar as he fails to reach it, he is discouraged with

self-pity, or plunged into despair. The only change that is
fitted to human nature is a forgiveness that only God can
supply, a new life that is a gift from God, a change wrought
in us by the Spirit Himself. Moral resolution dare not be
made, for it cannot possibly be fulfilled, without spiritual
regeneration. We must meet the approach of the Spirit in
our lives with welcome, with as much surrender as possible;
the fundamental work is done by Him in us. Do you know
that for an experience? Do you know that for such spiritual
change as has come to you, or must come to you, rests not
on your willpower nor resolve, but on what Christ gave you
by His life and by His death, the great truths of which the
Holy Spirit will enforce and illuminate and make personal
to you? Has a divine change come? Does it need to be completed? Does it need to be renewed? The Holy Spirit is the
Regenerator, the Giver of New Birth and New Life.

4. *The Holy Spirit is the Refresher.* And here I want you
to consider the real meaning of the word Comforter. The
Greek word *Paracletos* means someone who is called to our
aid, like a legal assistant, an advocate. The translation "Comforter," while containing a great truth and a great thought,
is soft: a Strengthener, or Refresher, would be better. One
thinks of Christ's own words, "Come unto Me, all ye that
labour and are heavy laden; and I will refresh you." Do you
know the thing that sleep can do for you when you are very
tired, that exercise and a good bath can do for you when
you have sat or worked too long in one place, or that a
change of scene does for you when you have gone stale?
This is just what the Holy Spirit does for our spirits. I think
of a man who has been living for years with negative
thoughts about himself: inferiority, self-hatred, condemnation of himself. We talked and then prayed and listened to
God, and the Holy Spirit gave him a succession of positive,
constructive thoughts which can be like a ladder for him out

of his discouragement. Think what the Holy Spirit gives to people who turn to Him when they are in trouble—the strong side of the word Comforter! I knew an artist advanced in years, who has lost both the sight of her eyes, and the full use of her hands, but she says she would lose them again a hundred times over for the spiritual victory that God's Spirit has given to her in these last years. If a man will turn to God and ask for help, there is no human need in which God cannot and will not help with the refreshment of the Holy Spirit.

5. *The Holy Spirit is the Reminder.* "He shall bring all things to your remembrance, whatsoever I have said unto you" (John 14:26). All of us treasure memories and sayings of people who have gone from us; and in the case of those who have made great contributions to the world, some summary of their wisdom is indispensable. Of course this was never so true of promise as in connection with the writing of the Four Gospels, "He shall . . . bring all things to your remembrance, whatsoever I have said unto you." The essential summary of His life, His acts, and the things He said, would be called into their minds by the Holy Spirit. We hear, and then what we hear sinks down into the subconscious memory. Have we filled our minds with His words so the Holy Spirit can call them up at any time, emphasize them, give the to us as corrective, encouragement, reminder?

But let us take this promise also in a wider sense, which accords with experience: the help of the Holy Spirit in cultivating a good memory. The first essential of memory is initial attention; and He will help us from wool-gathering when we should be listening to a name, or a fact. The next essential is that we be free from conflict, which is a breeder of forgetfulness; and He will take the conflict out of us. Persons most free from conflict may be those with the best memories. I am sure this is a gift of God. The Holy Spirit is the great Reminder.

6. *The Holy Spirit is the Revealer.* "The Spirit of truth . . . He shall teach you all things . . . He will teach you in that hour what ye shall say . . . He will guide you into all truth . . . He will show you things to come" (John 16:13). This means God speaking to the mind of man. Here is the long pursuit of truth, the slow, patient work of philosophers and scientists and artists: and all truth is God's truth. Here is also the promise of the ready word when it is needed in the spiritual warfare, "He will teach you in that hour what ye shall say." Do we depend on Him for that? Are we timid and afraid to give people our deepest convictions for fear they may ask us something we cannot answer? It is no substitute for thought and hard work, but it is rather rapid access to truth, which we know and need quickly.

"He will guide you into all truth"—suppose that became His arching motto for all education! Sometimes I think that, with all the good it has done, modern education has swelled our heads rather than filled them. Great teachers are first great learners. We can find knowledge, but we shall not find the wisdom we need until we look for it in the Spirit of truth. And "He will show you things to come." Do you believe that, and depend on it? Not satisfying selfish curiosity, but preparing those who need to know the turn of events, the course of affairs, if they are to do the maximum for God —yes, that is a very great experience. Divine warnings and encouragements are the heritage of those that keep close to the Holy Spirit.

7. *The Holy Spirit is the Rejoicer.* "And the disciples were filled with joy, and with the Holy Ghost." "Where the Spirit of the Lord is, there is liberty." A man told me that all his childhood memories of religion were gloomy. Gloomy religion may know moral principles, and theological truth, but gloomy religion never yet knew the Holy Spirit. There comes always, at Pentecost and always, a breeze when the Spirit

blows. The letter may kill, but the Spirit gives life—abundant life—always. Have you got so far yourself? I know plenty of people for whom religion means scruple, character, responsibility, and it is all fine. But what had happened when you can read, "The disciples were filled with joy, and with the Holy Ghost"? We can see at least these things that had happened; they had given their lives to God and were in control of His will and not their own; they found fellowship with one another; and they were full out in the adventure of bringing the world to their Master. That was their way to joy, and it is ours also. There is the sure mark of a church or a fellowship, a family or an individual, where the Holy Spirit is a reality: the presence of His joy.

8. *The Holy Spirit is the Remainer.* "He shall give you another Comforter, that he may abide with you forever" (John 14:16). And that means the Holy Spirit which was given on Pentecost to the family of Christ, the Church, has never been withdrawn. We give voice to the underlying faith that the Spirit is still with us when we pray, "Take not thy Holy Spirit from us." Has the Christian Church ever fully appreciated the gift of the Holy Spirit? We ask the Spirit's guidance in our ecclesiastical assemblies, in our worship, in our daily life: yet how many of us really believe that He can guide at all, how many of us listen to Him faithfully, and how many of us obey when He speaks? Imagine a Spirit-filled church, a fellowship inspired by Him at all times! He is the Remainer—He never gives us up, neither the Church, nor any one of us. Have we been disobedient, indifferent, inept, selfish? He still abides with us forever. Each of us knows how insistent is His coming and His convicting power. Actually we have never got so far away from Him that His voice is not still with us—the Holy Spirit, the Remainer, Who abides with us forever.

These, then, are some of the great realities about the Holy

Spirit, the Lord of Pentecost. He is the Reflector, the Re-prover, the Regenerator, the Refresher, the Reminder, the Revealer, the Rejoicer, and the Remainer.

And what shall we do about the Holy Spirit ourselves? We are told very distinctly to "grieve not the Spirit of God" (Ephesians 4:30), and to "quench not the Spirit" (I Thessalonians 5:9). We sometimes hear discussion of what the "sin against the Holy Spirit" is: Christ spoke of it in connection with the scribes who attributed the work of the Holy Spirit through Christ to Satan; that is, who denied His obvious presence and power. We deny them when we fail to recognize His work by its fruits (love, joy, peace, long-suffering, gentleness, goodness, faith, meekness, and temperance), and when we fail to look at Him and obey Him ourselves.

Let us pray, therefore, that the Holy Spirit may come to us this coming Pentecost as an abiding personal possession and power; as the Bringer of the wind and the fire of the Spirit to His Church; and through His Church, that He may bring light and unity to the world.

May God let it be so!

(Letter from Canon Shoemaker to the Rev. Dr. Henry Pitt Van Dusen, President Emeritus of Union Theological Seminary, New York.)

Pittsburgh, Pa
November 17, 1959

Dear Pitt:

I must tell you how thrilled I am with your book, *Spirit, Son and Father*. You have dared to see and point out, in the inner meaning of the New Testament, truths which are profoundly revolutionary, and which should be the focus of every contemporary Christian church, but are not.

The Church needs real guidance to recapture its lost

focus on the Holy Spirit because many in the conventional Church today cannot accept the implications of the Holy Spirit as presented by the so-called "Sects."

These more conventional people need the frame-work of stability and the historical knowledge of the past. Otherwise, they may be bereft of the Holy Spirit, and never meet Him, even in His own Church.

I am convinced after reading your book that we need a kind of ecumenical movement of the Spirit in the Church, with a glad recognition of His different forms and functions, but always the "same Spirit"!

As an example of the kind of thing I mean, we have just had a series of four talks on the Holy Spirit given by Dr. Charles Robshaw, a prominent Presbyterian minister, and sparked by our own Episcopal people. It has been a wonderful ecumenical venture, and Charles who is a great Spirit, has taken us into deep places and it has done us a world of good.

Forgive the length of this letter. I get carried away. I hope we may see each other before we are both too old to be able to see at all!

Yours Ever,
Sam

Canon Shoemaker's preoccupation with the Holy Spirit and His relevance to the Christian Church became almost an obsession during the last two years of his ministry. This preoccupation was sparked by reading Dr. Van Dusen's book, *Spirit, Son and Father,* and resulted in an unbroken sequence of months of preaching on different aspects of the Holy Spirit. Five of those sermons form Part III of this book, and out of the series came Canon Shoemakers own book on the Holy Spirit, *With the Holy Spirit and With Fire,* a best seller among religious books for many months.

CHAPTER 12

CHARISMATIC PEOPLE

"What we so-called Christians need is not more titillation and excitement in our religion for our own delectation, but we need a great awakening and conversion, and then a corresponding outpouring of our love for all the world, for the pagans at home and abroad. We need an encounter with the living Holy Spirit."

From
"Relish," Radio Address, 1962
By
Samuel Moor Shoemaker

What do you think is the greatest thing that can ever happen to a human being in this world? You might say that it is to find a great human love and to enjoy it all your life. You might say that it is to find a great task suited to your abilities and to give yourself to it with all your powers. You might even say that it is to experience a great spiritual awakening and conversion. But I think there is something beyond any of these.

What Is "Charisma"?

And I think that it is to become increasingly a charismatic person. What does this mean? The word "charis" in the New Testament is best rendered as "grace": the word "charisma" is best understood as a "gift of grace," a gift that is either stirred up or conferred by the coming into the life of "grace." And "grace," what is that? Grace technically means the merciful and unmerited kindness of God, especially as regards forgiveness and salvation; but it has come to mean the whole field of God's relation to us, His constant influence upon us, the helps of His Holy Spirit in daily life. A charismatic person, then, is one over whose whole life grace is poured out, and this grace affects others. It may manifest itself in some special gift like healing or spiritual influence. But the particular gift is often lost sight of in the consciousness that here we are in the presence of something which blesses, heals, restores, gives hope; and that this has come to be usually associated with the wonderful work of the Holy Spirit.

Not Just Belief Or Goodness

Do not confuse this with being theologically or even morally upright and correct. We have all seen people who believed all the right things, and followed the "straight and narrow," and they were as far from being charismatic as if they had been full-fledged pagans. The "good-will" people, the Sermon on the Mount and Golden Rule people, may or may not be charismatic people. How easily do some of these morally fine and theologically correct people become censorious and narrow, giving off nothing of the abounding grace and love and forgiveness of God, driving away the healing and transforming and reconciling powers which men need more than they need bread or sleep! You cannot "will" yourself into being a charismatic person, though you can use your will to keep yourself from being such a person; for it requires your consent. There is always a great, overall mercifulness about charismatic people. Self-righteousness cannot lie down in the same skin with this grace.

Holy Spirit Plus the Person

What causes this, then—is it a matter of personality? Yes, and no. A charismatic person is always a human personality in touch with the Holy Spirit. This need not be a brilliant personality; intellectual brilliance can be a deadly rival of the charismatic, though it is not always so. This need not be a bright and shining personality to begin with; rather does the charism bring brightness and shiningness into the otherwise drab and commonplace. The human personality involved here must be given rather than gifted, dedicated rather than highly endowed; but this dedication must not be of the straining, effortful variety, but rather of the gay and nonchalant variety, after the fashion of St. Francis of Assisi, who must have been one of the most charismatic men that ever lived, spreading the glamour of the grace of God wherever he went (I almost spelled that *h* in *he* with a Capital *H* so radiant and Christ-like was he!). It appears that God has hidden gifts within each of us which are meant to be stirred up when the Holy Spirit touches them; or else they are gifts that He brings with Him when He comes. It is this yielded, pliable, flexible, unselfconscious human personality given over in a glad kind of surrender to the Holy Spirit that produces a charismatic person. This can never be permanently resident in anybody, like the color of his eyes or the length of his legs: this is as dependent on current contact with the Holy Spirit as the light over your desk is dependent upon the immediate current of electricity. A given personality—of almost any old kind—plus the Holy Spirit, sought and found and sought again—this is what seems to create the charismatic personality.

The Condition of Willingness

I must say more of what "surrender" to the Holy Spirit

means in this case. Forget trying to be good, or believe all the right things, for the moment. Realize that God wants to come to you in abundance of pardon and mercy and grace, so that you are healed and whole again; and that He wants to pour out through you some of this grace to other people, especially in the ways associated with your personality. We can prevent this from happening by refusing to be a "fool for Christ's sake," to take a chance, to look a little absurd, to risk a failure, say at making a simple talk about what our faith means to us. Charismatic people keep seeking their steering directions from the Holy Spirit, not from the opinions of men. All kinds of fear are the deadly enemies of the charismatic, and we must let the charismatic drive them out or they will drive out the charismatic. There can be no coexistence between these two. The willingness to be used, to be an agent or instrument, to spread this radiance and joy, rather than try to accumulate it to ourselves, is the one sure way to find it. I suppose we musn't look too directly at the gift at all, or be too much concerned with whether we have it and give it or whether we don't. If we keep looking to the Holy Spirit for grace and direction, and to other people for their needs and hungers, we may slip into the position of mediation between them, and the current will begin to flow. This may far more often be the case with melted and even weak people than with frozen and strong ones. The morally self-righteous can hurt with their requisitions laid upon others. The charismatic seem to offer unknown and unrecognized possibilities which heal and do not hurt. The blazing eye and the clenched fist and the curled lip make poor companions for the charisma! But the sympathizing silence, the willingness not to have all the answers, the complete feeling of identity with others in all that they suffer—these make very good companions for the charisma!

Counterfeits

Now and then you will find either a professional charismatic or someone who seeks the gift for the power it bestows upon the possessor of it. You know about Simon in Acts 8: he saw the power of the Holy Spirit given through the laying on of the apostles' hands, and offered them money if they would give him this same power. And Peter had to say, "Thy silver perish with thee, because thou hast thought to obtain the gift of God with money. Thou hast neither part nor lot in this matter . . . Repent . . ." (Acts 8:20-22). Now there are people through whom it happens that a very continuous stream of power pours. They are not always people whom the orthodox churches approve of, but some of them are right within the orthodox churches. I suspect that these men and women have to exercise a very special care lest they treat the grace of God like a commodity that can be turned on like a faucet. I am sure they need again and again to surrender their gift to God, and to pray never to use it for their own gain or glory. We must beware of a reputation for spiritual power! I am sure that grace must ever be as fresh and current as electricity. For the electricity to be "on" means that power from the dynamo is continuously pouring out into and through the wires, "current" in both meanings of the word.

This Provokes Conviction of Sin

Now these charismatic people are the most moving, the most truly useful, in many ways the most attractive people in the world. But they are also among the most disturbing. For they give the patent lie to so much of the dead, respectable customs by which most of us run our lives. If they are right, we are wrong, and "the light that is in us is darkness." For they do not proceed by the intuitions and motions and inspirations of the Holy Spirit. Frequently they are really much smarter than the highly rational people, and more practical than the people whose stock-in-trade is thinking themselves practical. The charismatic has many a shortcut from sheer inspiration that the intellectual, the scientist, the rationalist knows nothing about. Hence these people bless those who receive them and their inspiration, but they cause conviction in those who reject them. Conviction of sin often arises most poignantly in us when we see in another the very quality we know should be in ourselves. Jesus was the most charismàtic person that ever lived, and shed about Him nothing but healing and love and truth and grace; yet the scribes and pharisees, the professional religious of His day, came to hate Him. Why? His life judged them. They ought to have been letting through the same kind of power but were not. It would be true to say that Jesus was crucified for being such a great charismatic. So do not be surprised if this provokes ridicule and hostility when you begin letting it happen through you.

Not long ago a worldly woman with a lifelong physical affliction was both converted and healed. Her family, her social-register friends were curious, skeptical, outraged. They taunted her, twitted her, but cannot let her alone, for there is the clear healing and the new life staring them in the face! She says, "My doctor says my health is perfect and will I wear a placard round my neck saying I am his patient. I smile and tell him he is wonderful (and he is) but I do not tell him he had very little to do with my new health." I suppose she does not feel he is ready for it yet nor can take the challenge of a healing that is charismatic in origin. You see, there is an antagonism, not only between the worldly and the spiritual people, but also between the conventionally religious and the charismatics. I think this woman probably has always had a great gift for spreading love and peace and healing. Now this has been hooked up with the Holy Spirit and the power is flowing. Some are glad and some are mad. Why is it so? I do not know, but it always is.

We have spoken at length, and not long ago, about the various gifts of the Holy Spirit. Already in the young Church these had emerged and they were found sufficiently repetitious to classify them—speaking in tongues, words of knowledge and wisdom, faith, healing, prophecy, discerning of spirits and of tongues. Some of these seem a little remote from us today; but some are as contemporaneous as Castro.

The Charisma of Healing

We all know the great new rise of healing movements. Some nonsense has been talked, some extravagant claims made; but that God does heal people through certain other people seems evident to an honest observer. While these healings are sometimes notably specific, I wish we might include within the great word "healing" those transformations of personality which take place deep in the subconscious, those which enable people to accept themselves without futile and unending guilt, reconciliation not only with others but with themselves and with life and with the world about them and with God. So many are uneasy, lonely, afraid. God seems very far from them. They may first know God as He shows Himself in the concern and healing power of another human being. For all the pride that lodges in the contemporary mind, what lodges much more often in the contemporary heart is loneliness and fear. You have met people that made you "feel good." This may have been more than a pleasant flash of cheer, this may have been that you were met by someone with a charisma of healing.

The Charisma of Spreading Faith

For others the gift is the impartation of faith. When you

come around such people, it is not that you shelve all your intellectual difficulties or maybe have them all answered, but rather that when you are with them you know that their possession of obvious radiant power is not an accident. They become themselves better arguments for faith than any the scholars can find. You do not so much learn faith from them as you catch it. You are drawn into sharing with them in such an experience as real prayer. Their spiritual essence pervades you, to use a phrase of Henry Drummond's. You do not so much come to believe intelligently in God or Christ or the Holy Spirit, as you begin having an experience of Him with someone who knows Him. It is not the arguments that convince us and get down to our roots, it is some almost irresistible gift that God has given them. They didn't especially try to convince us. They were themselves with us and let their faith manifest itself, and it drew us like a magnet.

Finally, do not put such people in a category from which you rule yourself out. Categories mean fences and fences mean exclusion, and there is no exclusion in God's great charismatic gifts, except the exclusion of those who exclude themselves . . . even God can't include them. When anyone thinks of himself or herself as belonging to some charismatic category, I suspect he will soon find himself outside it, unless he continuously comes back to the Holy Spirit for renewal and fresh grace. There are hidden gifts and spiritual possibilities within us all that go far beyond anything we have ever known; and the world is impoverished for the want of the manifestation of those same gifts. Don't strive to be a charismatic person, and for goodness' sake don't wear the heavenward look and the folded hands and the other fake poses of the fake spirituals. Let yourself go into the hands of God. Pray to Him to stir up the gifts He has given you. Pray it, not for your own satisfaction, but for His glory and for the needs of people about you and of all men everywhere. And in the next situation where you find yourself, let things begin to happen—and in the next, and in the next, till the Holy Spirit begins positively wearing a channel through you, and you are finding a meaning and a joy in living you never thought was possible this side of heaven!

"The best proof that we are influenced by the Spirit of God is, first, when the action itself is pure and conformable to the perfection of His laws. Secondly, when we perform it simply, tranquilly, without eagerness to do it, contented if it is necessary to relinquish it. Thirdly, when, after the work is done, we do not seek by unquiet reflections to justify the action even to ourselves, but are willing it should be condemned, or to condemn it ourselves, if any superior light discovers it to be wrong; and when, in fine, we do not appropriate the action to ourselves, but refer it to the will of God. Fourthly, when this work leaves the soul in its simplicity, in its peace, in its own uprightness, in humility, and in self-forgetfulness."

From
Selections From Fenelon
By Follen

(From letter from J. S. H. to the late
Dr. Samuel Moor Shoemaker)

Kansas City, Missouri
September 26, 1961

Dear Dr. Shoemaker:

Will it be possible for me to get ten copies of "Charismatic People?" I have need of this piece for a Home Study Group.

It is sad news, indeed, that you are going to have to discontinue "This Week's Word." This little pamphlet has brought "The Word" into the lives of thousands each week, in a vitalizing way. I am sure one of those and shall miss these sermons terribly.

Have you thought of putting these sermons into book form, or even making it possible to purchase them as a complete series? Those of us who have been receiving them in Kansas City believe that something along this line should be done because they represent too great a work to be lost except to those who have had the foresight to file them.

With sincere gratitude for all that "This Week's Word" has meant to so many,

Gratefully,
J. S. H.

(From letter to Mrs. O. after Canon Shoemaker died)
Kansas City, Mo.
February 14, 1964

Dear Mrs. O:

Thank you for writing me of Dr. Shoemaker's death. The sermons he mailed to me and thousands of others, called "T.W.W.," are used by many I know in Kansas City yet.

The one I remember especially and have used in groups and individual counseling is called "Charismatic People." Of course, there are others, but this one was so helpful that I asked Doctor Shoemaker for extra copies. I have not a single copy left because I have found so many for whom that sermon was just right to meet a need.

Occasionally one's path is crossed by that of an individual who obviously has been given of these charismatic qualities, but seems totally unaware of this themselves. I recall such a young woman in New York to whom I sent this sermon, and this is a line from the letter she wrote: "I was lonely and lost in this vast place, and then came your letter with the enclosure of 'Charistmatic People.' I have read and re-read it and begin to feel sure of God again, and have started to go out to people instead of withdrawing from them. It works wonders, and thank you for sending me that wonderful help. It said just what I needed to hear."

Of course, I was delighted, and I have found many times that when this particular piece is used to waken realization of the Holy Spirit as a living Person, that always response is spontaneous and lasting.

Dr. Shoemaker himself had this gift in great measure, but with the quiet revelation in his own life which is the sign of authenticity.

I read a quotation from Dr. Albert Schweitzer the other day which made me think of Dr. Shoemaker. It goes like this:

"Just as the water of the streams we see is small in comparison to that which flows underground, so the idealism which becomes visible is small in amount compared with what men and women have locked in their hearts, unreleased or scarcely released. To unbind what is bound, to bring the underground waters to the surface, mankind is waiting and longing for such as can do that."

And this is what Dr. Sam did for untold numbers of people. He had a rare gift of helping people to realize a potential they never knew they had. Would that there were more like him!

I will look forward to the book.

Sincerely,
J. S. H.

CHAPTER 13

THE SUREST MARK
OF A CHRISTIAN

"GOODNESS"

"All goodness, if it's true, is passion-filled
Buoyant and radiant, with the whole soul willed.
Bring to it then, an unwithholding mind,
And touch it with the love of humankind . . . .
So with unstudied art thy soul shall tell
The joy of living eagerly, and well!"

From
So I Stand By The Door and Other Poems
By
Samuel Moor Shoemaker

What would you say is the surest mark of a Christian?
You might say that faith is, or that love is. And there would
be truth in both statements. But I am going to give you
another that I think is even more the surest mark of a person who has found what Jesus Christ came on earth to have
him find.

It is joy!

Have We a Right To Joy?

Now some very good and conscientious person may want to contradict me at the very outset, and say, "What right has anyone calling himself a Christian to be joyous? He lives in a world filled with starvation-hunger, clouded with fear, and full of strife within human personality and outside it. Millions know nothing of a God of love. What right have we, in our comfortable condition, to talk about joy?"

And that sounds very plausible. And if our joy meant indifference to human tragedy, we would better be done with it. But what if our joy arose out of the fact that we believe we have discovered something that is a remedy for the suffering and fear and pain of the world? And what if our joy itself were part of the medicine with which God is trying to cure the sickness of the world?

Christ: Joy

Nobody ever lived that was more burdened with the tragedy and desperation of human life than Jesus. Yet he counselled joy, and promised it: "These things have I spoken unto you, that my joy may be in you, and that your joy may be full" (John 15:11, RSV). And what of Jesus Himself? G. K. Chesterton closes one of his greatest books, and one of the greatest pieces of Christian apologetic of our time, the one called *Orthodoxy*, with these words: "There was something that He hid from all men when He went up a mountain to pray. There was something that He covered constantly by abrupt silence or impetuous isolation. There was some one thing that was too great for God to show us when He walked upon our earth; and I have sometimes fancied it was His mirth." That I think to be inspired insight. For He was a "Man of Sorrows" only in that He felt the sorrow of the world and shared in it by His own sacrifice. But you cannot tell me that either little and guileless children, or old and guilty men and women, would have found Him so irresistible in His interest in them had He not been also a Man of Joy.

Religion Without Joy—A Betrayal

Have not whole sections of His people almost completely misunderstood Him and His religion? Of course religion is serious business, but surely this does not mean that religion is sobersided and solemn business! It seems to me more and more that almost the whole Puritan strain, together with its descendants in every age is—but for its effort towards discipline—a bad counterfeit of the Christian religion. I see no place in it, either for the judgmental hardness towards the sins of human weakness, nor for the joylessness of men who divest themselves of happiness in the name of God. I think they are wrong—a thousand times wrong! I do not think Jesus was like that for one moment. When we are like this, either we have not discovered the profound joy that belongs to forgiven and redeemed people, or we have failed to realize what a terrible injustice we are doing Christ by appearing so joyless about our religion, to other people.

Dr. Paul Tillich might be expected to have spoken to this point, and he has, "Is our lack of joy due to the fact that we are Christians, or to the fact that we are not sufficiently Christian? . . . The suppression of joy, and guilt about joy in Christian groups, almost drove me to a break with Christianity. What passes for joy in these groups is an emaciated, intentionally childish, unexciting, unecstatic thing without color and danger, without heights and depths." No more serious thinker nor believer walks in our world. But he was almost lost to the Christian cause by cheerless Christians, or Christians whose cheer was of the cheap, meaningless variety that puts on a smile and talks with false glee.

And let me give you another instance of the poor effect of cheerless religion. Dr. Charles W. Eliot, when he was president of Harvard, was once in church in London. He wrote home to his son, "Yesterday we attended M.'s church, heard an excellent sermon, badly delivered. The whole service lacked cheerfulness. The tones of M's voice and his inflections were all depressing. It is almost the worst of faults in a preacher. Faith, hope, and love are all cheerful things and ought to be made to appear so by those who preach them. Life is not always bright, but religion should be."

Christian Joy: Not Pretense, Nor Mere Health

Now there is one thing sure and certain: this kind of joy is not something you can put on or pretend. This comes up out of you because it is in you, or else you cannot show it. Someone said to me of a man we both knew that "he smiled with his lips, but not with his eyes." You know when a person, desperately trying to convince you of being a thoroughly devoted Christian, puts on the forced smile and talks in a sentimentally positive way. Christian joy is something you can't fake. It is a sure mark that the Lord is dealing with you He may be dealing with you with discipline which you may not especially enjoy; but what you enjoy is the fact that He is in your life and you are working with Him and walking with Him.

Another thing we must notice. Christian joy is different from a naturally cheerful disposition, which may be due to strong health or good glands. Let us not belittle either one. But Christian joy can exist in people who are not naturally exuberant, and in people who do not have great physical vitality. I think their Christian faith will give them something to be exuberant about, and I think it will add to their physical vitality. But spiritual joy is a spiritual gift, not a by-product of mere physical health. I have seen it in people who were suffering intensely in body, and sometimes in people who were suffering intensely in mind and spirit. There may be something less than gayety under these conditions; but they will have in their sorrow, or pain, or bafflement, a quiet assurance of God being with them, of His strength and His grace, which is the surrogate of Christian joy for suffering and tried people. Even when it speaks in a muffled tone, it is worth a thousand times more than the pretended gladness of the professional religious cheermonger.

The Source of Christian Joy

Why are Christians joyful? Surely not because the world is a perfect enough place to call for no concern on our part. Surely not because we can shut out its anguish from our hearts and be left in peace. Still less that we are doing so well ourselves that we can settle down in complacency and be satisfied. I fear we often look for our bastard joy in these evasive and counterfeit things. But they are not even distant relatives of Christian joy.

Man's Desperation

Christian joy comes, as I see it, from just one thing and that is gratitude. And the gratitude arises out of an overwhelming need which has been met by a staggering answer. Most of us are so comfortable that we see neither the need nor the contrast, and therefore cannot feel the joy. Man's natural state is an animal state, with a horrible gnawing nostalgia for a God Whom he has lost. We find ourselves in a world with no maps nor clues. There is no telling (by our own wisdom) whence we came, what we are supposed to be doing here, nor what happens to us when we depart. We are not nice civilized people learning to become all the

while more civilized; we are lost men and women, blind
to how lost we are because we have so much of this world's
goods and activity and pleasure to bemuse us. We take
most of our light from other human beings as lost as we
are ourselves. We face a life with no built-in values, no
known significance; and after this an unknown eternity or
nothingness. We do not see the issues of life clearly enough
to be intelligently religious, or even to be intelligent—
"period." Matthew Arnold was not just enjoying a pessimistic
rhapsody—rather was he describing the human situation
when he wrote, in "Dover Beach,"

> .... the world which seems
> To lie before us like a land of dreams,
> So various, so beautiful, so new,
> Hath really neither joy, nor love, nor light,
> Nor certitude, nor peace, nor help for pain;
> And we are here as on a darkling plain
> Swept with confused alarms of struggle and flight,
> Where ignorant armies clash by night.

Redemption

My friends, it is not just a few ethical rules that I need
to guide me in a world like this; I need some clue to the
meaning of what the world is, and what life is, and what
I am. The people who think that the chief contribution of
Jesus to human life is the precepts which He taught have
neither understood life nor Him. He came to tell us what is
the meaning of the world and life and man himself by telling
us of God, a God Whom man has somehow rejected but
cannot forget, a God Who created the universe and life for
a purpose, a God Who in condescending pity saw man's
predicament and sent His Son into the world to live as
life should be lived, to die on a Cross for man's redemption,
and to rise again from the dead in sign of God's full and

final triumph over sin and death. Christ is wisdom for our unknowing. He is company for our loneliness. He is meaning for our purposelessness. He is balm for our grief and peace for our pain. He has come to us and given Himself to us. He is our answer, for He came from Beyond. There are not a thousand lights on this "darkling plain"—there is really only One that I can find Who can speak for God because He is God.

His coming is our source of gratitude, and our gratitude is the source of our joy for nothing in this world is so selflessly joyful as gratefulness. You will never really feel this unless you see the Christian answer set over against the complete confusion and ultimate despair of man left to himself as he finds himself. The world itself is actually much more like that little boy that was lost, imprisoned, suffocating and dying down that well shaft a few weeks ago, than it is like its own false picture of itself as—given education and science—quite capable of saving itself. Somebody had to come after that little fellow who could not extricate himself from his predicament, and dig away the imprisoning earth, and set him free. Somebody has to come after us who cannot extricate ourselves from our prison house of sin and unknowing and meaninglessness, and set us free. If you can imagine the difference in the way that little lad viewed his life before the experience of the well, and how he viewed it afterwards, you will have some notion of what it is we enjoy in Christian redemption. It is literally the difference between life and death.

Daily Joy

But there is a current and daily footnote to this great, over-arching joy of the Christian redemption. And that is found in the awareness that God is at work in our lives and concerned for our daily decisions. He has a plan for us, and He will help us to find it step by step as we are obedient to the light we have. God seems to have respect for man's freedom and not to thwart our power to disobey Him and get into trouble. But there is a plan and, when we follow it, we discover God's unmistakable Providence in our lives. That plan is made plain to us in the Bible, and it is also revealed to us as we pray seeking His will rather than our own. If we know nothing of any feeling that God is at work in us and with us, it is probable that we have not given enough of our wills to Him so that He can work without trespassing on our freedom, or that we do not pray enough. Prayer must always be seeking to find His will, not to change it.

When we honestly leave things to God, being willing only to obey as we think He is telling us to do, we are aware of helps, encouragements, pieces of guidance, "coincidences," which are too frequent and too obvious to be accidents. This can lie close to superstition, and the experience of it can endanger us with the sin of pride. But I can introduce you to a hundred people in whose lives things like this are of common enough occurrence so that they would not be at a loss to give you an instance of them of fairly recent date. And it is not spiritual pride and self-assurance that marks these people, it is rather a kind of surprised joy that God is perceptibly real in life, and that they are finding it possible to work with Him. When you get out into the mid-stream of this kind of living, your whole life begins to feel like a continuous adventure, broken sometimes by your own disobedience, but resumed when you tell God you are really sorry. He seems to take up with you again with surprising readiness, and begin again to help you to live and make decisions. The word "enthusiasm" means being "in God"; for whom religion is so real that it is always more or less exciting. Even when its music is in a minor key, when we are in great human difficulty, or suffering, the same unearthly joy is there. One of the saints of God whom I have known was knocked down by a balloon tire that flew off a truck passing by and broke her hip. I saw her soon after in a hospital, in traction and in great pain. With a selfless kind of smile she said to me, "I wonder what God has for me to do here!" And one thing was the conversion of a skeptical trained nurse who read her Bible to her, and began to catch her faith. That kind of almost unbroken, indomitable, adventurous faith gives people the only joy that the world cannot give nor take away.

And this joy is the surest mark of a Christian!

"Christ will not make life easy. He will make it great. As you walk with Him, He will fill your heart with a thankfulness that is overflowing, and a joy that this world can neither give nor take away,

Christian joy is a by-product of loving God."

From
The Enjoyment of God
By
Samuel Moor Shoemaker

(From letter to the late Canon Shoemaker from the Rev. C. S. Chaplain)

Dutchess County, N. Y.
July 24, 1960

Dear Sam:

As I read your sermon "The Surest Mark of a Christian," I remember something you said once before, namely that we never know how deep is a Christian's joy until you see him in a situation which causes other people acute misery.

This leads me to ask you to mail "T.W.W." to a young woman here at Millbrook County Home, Miss Louise T.

Miss T. has been bedfast now for nearly twenty years, and still is the most radiant Christian I know.

She will not only find great help in your sermons of T.W.W. but will share them with many others. I wish you and Louise could know each other, as you are kindred spirits.

Thank you for "T.W.W." in the name of many of our people.

Faithfully,
C. S.

(From letter written four years later to
Mrs. O. from the Rev. C. S.)

Scarboro, Ontario
September, 1964

Dear Mrs. O:

Thank you for the opportunity you have provided Louise T. and me to do our small part in memory of our beloved Dr. Sam.

Lately, when I was in Dutchess County at the Home where Louise still is, I told her of the book you are putting together of Dr. Sam's sermons. She was delighted and will write you later. But, as an example of a truly joyous Christian, maybe you would like to hear something about this woman.

I met her first in 1960 during a series of services I conducted at the Millbrook County Home. During the two and one half years I knew her after that, before I moved here to Scarboro, she gave constant and radiant witness to her love of God every moment of the day. Louise is a victim of arthritis. Her fingers are too twisted for her to write, so she has asked me to write the enclosed letter for her, which she has dictated to me.

Again, thank you for letting us say how much we owe to Sam, and how much we love him.

Very sincerely,
C. S.

(From letter enclosed by the Rev. C. S. to Mrs. C.C.O. dictated by L. T.)

Dutchess County, N. Y.
September 11, 1964

Dear Mrs. O:

All the sermons of T.W.W. which I received had some special help which I always seemed to be needing. I have most of them, and they are marked at the sentences that meant so much to me, and I read them again and again, and pass them on to someone else who is in need of spiritual strength and comfort. I have been told by many that the sermons have meant the same to others that they have to me.

The sermons on the Holy Spirit, and those on Prayer, have assisted greatly in my spiritual growth and strengthening my Christian conduct day by day.

I miss the sermons coming each week, and by all means do put some of them into a book so that others may read them and be given the strength and patience and love they need in such places as hospitals, etc.

These sermons should not be lost, even though Dr. Shoemaker has gone.

Lovingly and gratefully,
L. T.

(From letter to Mrs. C.C.O. from C.L., Jr.)

Scarsdale, New York
February 13, 1964

Dear Mrs. O:

It was good of you to write to us with news of the late
Canon Shoemaker's death. We are glad that you are trying
to find a way for Canon Shoemaker's influence to continue.
I am sure that it has been greater than anyone can reckon.

The little folder came to my family each week, and the
day was eagerly anticipated, for all of us, from the young-
est on up, found in these sermons unique honesty, humility,
and, above all, joy which is truly the surest mark of a
Christian.

I remember so many of the sermons, or bits of them, and
one in which Dr. Shoemaker told the story of a woman who
had a terrible accident and was taken to the hospital, and
almost on arrival said, "Well, I wonder what God has for
us to do here?"

The story goes on to say that since the elderly woman
could not read lying on her back she asked her nurse to
read the Bible to her. The nurse was a skeptic, herself, but
the quiet joy of this Christian in the midst of disaster convinced the nurse at last that there was some connection between 'the joy this woman was able to reflect and the
truths she read aloud from the Bible. At last the nurse
came into a close knowledge of Christ and became, herself,
a joyous Christian.

There were always such pertinent stories woven into Dr.
Shoemaker's sermons. But if I tried to enumerate all the
strength, depth, balance, and joyous conviction about life
and enthusiasm for it which I received as I read these
sermons, this would be much too long a letter.

Suffice it to say that we look forward to the book with
keen anticipation even though we have kept many of the
sermons from T.W.W. and read them from time to time
even yet.

Thank you for writing to us about your project.

Sincerely,
G. L., Jr.

CHAPTER 14

THE HOLY SPIRIT
IN THE LIFE OF THE CHURCH

"It must be perfectly obvious that what the whole Church needs from top to bottom is a deeper conversion, a profounder experience of the Holy Spirit."

From
This Week's Word
By
Samuel Moor Shoemaker

Pentecost is often spoken of as the "birthday of the Church." This has always seemed to me both true and false—false because our Lord had certainly called out His disciples and formed them into an organic unity and fellowship long before Pentecost; and true because the full meaning of their mission, and especially the power that had been given to them to carry it out, seems to have first really been given to them at Pentecost. Ever since then it has been more or less impossible to speak about the Church without speaking about the Holy Spirit, or to speak about the Holy Spirit without speaking about the Church.

Church Is Where the Holy Spirit Is

In some churches the Holy Spirit is spoken of as if He

were the sole possession of the Church, indeed the Church's
Creature, Who is to be found nowhere else than in the
Church. Then the question arises, "What Church is the au-
thentic Church?" And while men bicker and dispute about
this, the Holy Spirit jumps the traces and turns up somewhere the ecclesiastics think He shouldn't be. Few are so
blasphemous and self-righteous as to refuse to see His foot-
print anywhere but in their own Church. But we had better
turn things around where they belong. We do not find the
Holy Spirit only where the Church is; rather we find the
Church only where the Holy Spirit is, as Irenaeus said centuries ago.

We must always remember that faith in the Holy Spirit
(as in the Trinity) came out of an experience. A group of
theologians did not lock themselves in a room and come
up with the idea of Three Persons and One God. Men experienced God as Creator, as Saviour, and as Empowerer;
yet these were not three gods but One God. The experience
of the Holy Spirit was an extension of the experience of
Christ, yet it was different. This Presence and Power that
came to them at Pentecost was a new experience.

Early Christian Experience

The Christian religion, as first experienced in the early
Church, was of a nature not easily described. It did not consist principally of theological convictions, though these are
there. It did not consist in seeking to live a life of righteousness, though its adherents undoubtedly did so. The nature
of that early experience was more like stepping into a stream
of power, and being borne along in it. Miraculous things
happened to and through them, but they were not the
doers of them. They had an amazing unity, in spite of
sharp disagreements at times. It must have been exciting in
the extreme to be in their midst. One never knew when

somebody would start speaking in tongues, or another would begin to tell of his newfound faith in Christ. There seem to have been always two kinds of gathering: the formal kind, where a liturgy based on the events at the time of the original Lord's Supper guided them to perform the service much the same way each time; and the informal kind, which was not so much like our Morning Prayer as like an experience meeting, with a good deal of spontaneous participation by the people. To the first, only the initiated were invited. To the second, enquirers as well as believers were welcome. The power that came to them from the Holy Spirit in both kinds of meetings seemed to continue with them when they separated.

The Cycle of Power

But in time disorder appeared in both services requiring greater control. And within a relatively few years these fires had burned very low. There seems to be a usual cycle in the experience of the Holy Spirit in the Church. First, a group of people begins gathering for prayer and for fellowship. They are being made ready for the coming of the Holy Spirit. At some point His Presence is unmistakably made known, and His power enjoyed for a season. Then this time of intense creative renewal is followed by one of gradually diminishing vigor, with the emphasis placed more and more upon theological and organizational rigidity. This continues until the human need and the divine readiness meet again in renewal. Dr. E. F. Scott tells us that belief in the Holy Spirit was grounded in certain experiences, and in the religion of the later age these had become unusual and to a great extent unreal: and he says that when the ecclesiastical idea had begun to overshadow all Christian thought, the belief in the Spirit tended to disappear, or to have a merely formal value.

Dr. Henry P. Van Dusen, in the book *Spirit, Son and Father*, traces in outline what he calls "the fate of the Holy Spirit at the hands of the theologians and the Church officials across the centuries," calling it "on the whole a pathetic and tragic story." These are the steps and stages:

The indubitable centrality of the Holy Spirit in the life and message of the earliest Church.

Its regnancy in the faith and thought of the Apostle Paul.

Its capture and imprisonment by Catholic ecclesiasticism.

Its release and renewal in every epoch of spiritual revival.

Its re-imprisonment by the classic Reformers within the text of Scripture.

Its emancipation with power by the so-called "Radical Reformation," the "Reformation Sects."

Its gradual quiescence into innocuous conventionality in their later respectability.

Today, its reappearance in familiar excess and wonted power in the contemporary "sects."

Holy Spirit and the Ecclesiastics

He declares that "professional ecclesiasts constitutionally distrust the novel, the unconventional, and even more, the reproachful and the challenging . . . They may seek to discredit and disown what they distrust, as did Amos and Micah; or they may accomplish the same end by taking the troublesome disturber under their patronage and emasculating it through redefinition and regulation." One cannot but think of what the Roman Church did to St. Francis and his movement; and of the high-handed Pharisaism and folly of our own Church towards John Wesley. "But," says Dr. Van Dusen, "the Holy Spirit has always been troublesome, disturbing because it has seemed to be unruly, radical, unpredictable . . . embarrassing to ecclesiasticism and baffling to ethically-grounded, responsible durable Christian devotion. And so it has been carefully taken in hand by Church authorities, whether Catholic or Protestant, and securely tethered in impotence. But—the Spirit will not long be silenced. When neglected or denied by the prevailing 'churchianity,' it unfailingly reappears to assert its power, often with excesses and aberrations, beyond the bounds of conventional Church life."

It looks to me as if only the most hardy and courageous beginnings of renewal have ever survived the first cold storms of disapproval which the conventional Church has showered again and again on these tiny, green shoots. One wonders how many of them have perished along the way of the centuries, destined for great good and mighty results, but nipped off early by frightened bureaucrats to whose interest it was to confine the Holy Spirit to the practices of the Church or the words of the Bible. These preservers of ecclesiastical order can always find human faults and frailties in the men whom the Spirit was using in these beginnings—no greater than those of the ecclesiasts themselves, if we are truthful. But it is easy to hide our own fears under scorn for spiritual upstarts, forgetful that the Spirit may be more nearly present with the start than with the hierarchy. I saw at least one spiritual awakening among students hamstrung and destroyed by clergy of one of our great churches; and as I look back on it, I am quite sure that fear and jealousy and a merely nominal faith in the Holy Spirit were what really underlay their action. It well may be that the Church itself has more than once destroyed the first signs of an awakening for which the Church was itself fervently praying. The Holy Spirit does not work as men work.

The Small Group and the Holy Spirit

Our instant need, in this day, is to draw more people, and more groups of people, into that stream of power which is the life of the Holy Spirit in the Church and in the world. This means the Church must begin to do again what once it did, and that is to seek the conversion of individuals to Christ that through Him they may come to know the Holy Spirit. And it means that the Church must learn to do something which it has only intermittently known in the past, and that is how to conduct the kind of small gatherings in which people can be exposed to those dynamic truths of the Gospel which lead into an experience of Christ and of the Holy Spirit. Our preaching and teaching alone do not by any means always do this.

Organism, Not Organization

Let me be very personal and describe to you how such a group gets under way. In my parish we had a rather weak young adult group. I knew some of them were not such young men and women as you could build on. We waited till about eight or ten appeared who might become the nucleus of a possible group. Week after week I met with them myself. Then for a succession of weeks we exposed them to young married couples in whose lives Christ had begun to work; these encounters did not consist of speeches but of witness, the sharing of experience. Most people have heard Christian truth, few of them have been exposed to Christian experience, as alcoholics in A.A. are exposed to the processes which lead to sobriety. The ten young adults began to try this themselves: to pray, to face up to the surrender of themselves to Christ, the living out of Christian faith day by day, the witness to their friends. They have worked out a program of meetings which include three kinds of talks: (1) on the intellectual problems of doctrine; (2) on the practical expression of Christian faith in needed human service; (3) the witness of experience. Now they are ready to expand, begin bringing in more people, offering more kinds of healthy social life, multiplying small groups within the larger one for more intensive fellowship and prayer.

Such a group is much more an organism than an organization. An organism can clothe itself with an organization, and function through it; but an organization is never any substitute for an organism. I do not think the Holy Spirit finds organizations always easy to work through; but an organism, where life touches life, in witness, in fellowship and in prayer, seems to give to Him what a wire gives to electricity —a channel through which to come. Of course nothing takes the place of prayer and concern; these must always underlie such small groups. Someone gets on fire, and the fire touches someone else, and so organically the group gets going. This is, of course, not the only means the Holy Spirit uses in the Church today. He uses great evangelists and preachers, He uses good and solid teaching, He uses services of worship and of Sacraments. But there are literally thousands in our churches who, if they were honest, would say what a man in my congregation said to me awhile ago, "I have been coming to this church for forty years, and I still don't know what it's all about." Such foreshortened exposure to dynamic truth and personalities in the crucible of growing experience is one of the ways He uses to come into the life of individuals and of the Church.

Let me tell you the story of one person in that group, and then of a visit some of the group made so as to get going a youth group in another place.

This young man has been more or less in touch with the Church throughout his life. He made a Christian decision in college, and did a lot of Christian work there. But something still held him back. He has always felt that in some way God was pursuing him, and at times he has all but cursed God to His face for His persistence. He graduated from a large state university, and went to work for a great company. While in training, he heard a talk given the trainees—a captive audience at 8:30 on a weekday morning, about spiritual awakening and its utter necessity if the values we believe in are to survive. He sought the speaker out. In prayer he made a further Christian decision. He came spiritually alive in a new way. He cannot find enough to read. His prayers are positively exciting to him. He has witnessed to many of his friends, and they have become interested and some have come into the stream with him. He talked about this with a girl friend of his, and she was surprised to find so intelligent a person as he, using his mind as well as his heart, in faith and powerful influence over people.

Extending the Stream

We were asked by a neighboring church to bring some of our young people, and help them start a young adult group. We took along four of them, first giving a picture of what life in the stream of the Holy Spirit is like, and then calling on these four one by one to speak out of their own experience. Do you realize how much more effective it is when people hear these things, not in general from a minister, but directly from lay people their own age and general situation speaking personally from experience? That evening another fellow sat and listened; and when our team was through speaking, he opened up on his own situation—fine family background, fine school, Harvard University, a job in a family bank. But he knew he was missing something. Let me give this to you in a letter he sent me:

"Both of my college roommates with whom I grew up had something that I wanted but felt I couldn't have, because attaining it would be too costly. What my roommates had was Christ, and through Him they were happy and satisfied with life. Both talked to me many times, and I admit they influenced me, but I was still concerned about the cost. My idea of the cost was giving up my friends, social life, and self-reliance. It was my contention that people who turned to God were weaklings. Look at the ministers and missionaries—seldom did they have good looks! I'd have sworn that one entered the ministry because he could not have been successful anywhere else. But still something was drawing me because I kept on going to church, kept in touch with my Christian roommates, and finally ended up helping start a Youth Group in our church. When I talked with you I was surprised to find how simple yet difficult it was to ask God to take over the reins—simple because it seemed as if there was no other logical choice, difficult because I was still worried about the cost. That worry ended after the prayer we had together. Since then I have discovered that the costs I was worried about are not costs at all. I still have my friends (have started to work on a few of them). But more important, I have found new friends who are true friends . . . I have never felt so close to my family and can never tell you the joy when I gave my girl her ring in front of both our families . . . I loved my job at the bank before I found the Lord, now even more so. My ability to learn the job seems to increase. It's funny to look at the things that hold a person from God, and then look what happens when God is asked to take you over . . . Our group is going along wonderfully. We have settled down to a group of about eleven, and are now studying The Acts. We have a real Christian helping us. I am learning a great deal and it gives me a nightly project, as well as prayer. My girl says if I gave as much time to my accounting books as I do to The Acts I might learn the difference between a debit and a credit."

So does a real stream overflow its banks and start another stream. So do individual men and women come down off the banks of self-centered, materialistic, unsatisfying, stupid living, and get into the stream themselves. Give us hundreds of them, thousands of them, millions of them, all across the world—and the Holy Spirit will start a flood of power and forgiveness and reconciliation that will change the face of the earth! But it begins with me and with you.

"What we need is a great sweeping movement of the Holy Spirit, bigger than any of us, bigger than any church or all of them taken together, including (please God) but transcending us all."

From
With The Holy Spirit and With Fire
By Samuel Moor Shoemaker

(From letter to the late Canon Shoemaker from a minister in India)

Calcutta, India
October 13, 1960

Dear Dr. Shoemaker:

I have been reading "This Week's Word" since a friend entered my name on your mailing list some months ago. I am so enthusiastic about its value to ministers that I want to share some of the ones I have been helped by with the ministers at Clergy Conference in Calcutta which is coming in the Spring.

Can you let me have fifty copies of "The Holy Spirit In the Life of the Church"? That is a good many to ask for, but I will gladly pay the costs as this sermon has meant so very much to me in my own effort to preach on this subject. Many of us here wonder about the Church's real mission and how well, or badly, it is being performed, and I gather you are aware of the poverty of life in the Church many times.

I wish I could meet you, or that you could be at a conference that I could attend, but, of course, that is not possible. I do thank you with my whole heart for your splendid sermons.

Faithfully,
T. M.

(From letter written to the late Canon Shoemaker from a Presbyterian missionary in South Africa)

Durban, South Africa
June, 1961

Dear Dr. Shoemaker:

All the sermons of the series on the Holy Spirit have been read with even more interest than the others I've had from "T.W.W." I am sure that is because only from His Spirit can one receive the courage and the strength to do our almost impossible task here in this torn and deeply troubled land.

If the Holy Spirit did not sustain us we could not go on. God bless you for your world concern for all men everywhere, and for your honesty and concern for the Church as it is in too many places. You are not critical so much as concerned. There are always critics of the Church, but most of them do nothing to try to make the Church more as it was in the beginning, a loving body with Christ at the head of all.

I'd like to talk to you, but it is wonderful to have "T.W.W."

Gratefully,
M. B.

(From letter to C.C.O. from C.V. after Canon Shoemaker died)

Huntsville, Alabama
January 20, 1964

Dear Mrs. O:

It was a delight to have word that you are planning a collection of Dr. Sam's sermons from "T.W.W." because I owe those sermons my own understanding of the Church and the Spiritual truths which they taught me.

I first met Dr. Sam when I was very much of a child. He preached a series of sermons at our Church, and because I was planning then to be a medical missionary I attended every service and talked with Dr. Sam about all this..

I corresponded with Dr. Sam on this subject, and, looking back, I wonder how he had time or patience to give me so much of his time, but he did and never made me feel that my questions, observations, etc. were not important.

Then later I met his daughter, Nickie, and visited them in their home in Pittsburgh, and there, too, Dr. Sam took time to talk to me about my plans.

Then came college, and I went through the usual doubts and mistakes of judgment, and soon I felt the Church did not live up to its words and stopped going entirely but I did read Dr. Sam's sermons as he sent me "T.W.W." every week that whole first year.

I remember the one which talked about how people criticize the Church, yet do nothing about making it better, and how they are the *real* hypocrites, and I began to see the light.

But still I often thought that it was an impossible and senseless task to attempt to work out any kind of Christian life where everything was so different from home, and no one seemed to think it important. No one but Dr. Sam. He still wrote to me.

Well, I am married now, and have a baby, and the dream of being a missionary was only a dream, I guess. But I know that all my life will be better because Dr. Sam took time for me and sent me "T.W.W." while I was in college, where life was no picnic, as I remember it now.

Thank you for letting me express my gratitude to Dr. Sam; I grieve for his death.

Sincerely,
(Mrs.) C. V.

CHAPTER 15

ETERNAL LIFE

"When we honestly seek to make God, His will and His Kingdom central, there is a quiet assurance that there is nothing to fear either about physical dying or about what lies beyond."

Samuel Moor Shoemaker

By far the greatest gift that is promised to Christian believers in the revelation brought by Christ is the gift of eternal life. We are all, quite naturally, and perhaps quite rightly, concerned immediately with this life here and now. Most of us are more or less western "activists," and we are fairly healthy-minded with no morbid interest in death. But if the Christian faith is true, and we are promised that in Christ we shall live forever, then this concerns, not these few fleeting years here, with inevitably so much of darkness and suffering, but an eternity without number of years and with joy and bliss. No matter how busy we are, we must remember that, if we survive death at all, by far the greater part of life, both for duration and for intensity, lies on the "other side."

The Human Longing for Immortality

I can understand it if a person says, "I wish I could believe all this, for it would be comforting, but I can't." I do not think it an easy thing to believe in eternal life. There seems to be an ending to the things we see in nature—not the sleep of winter in the flowers and trees, but the death which puts an end to life altogether. Man belongs in part to nature. Some will feel that he comes to a full end also. I can understand a person having suffered so much, mentally or physically, that they may say in a momentary protest, "I have had enough. The relief of oblivion would be welcome." But this represents a mood, not a considered attitude. I cannot understand anyone not caring, or pretending not to care, whether this all may be fulfilled for their loved ones or for them. And if there is even a chance that such a thing may exist, I cannot understand their living as if they were indifferent to it, as if there were nothing they needed to do to prepare for it. There is many a long sea-mile of difference between being blotted out, like an ant you step on as you tread the sidewalk, and the Christian promise of eternal life!

Let me say that the word "immortality" is used, but it is much less used in the New Testament than the words "eternal" or "everlasting life," which seem to mean the same thing.

It is perfectly clear that the words refer to a definite personal survival after death. Some people mean by immortality that their memories survive. We recall them. Their influence goes on, in their children and descendants, and in the people whose lives they affect. This only postpones somewhat longer the day when no one is left who remembers them. Go into any cemetery you like, and consider the names engraved on pretentious monuments which never were an appropriate memorial for a Christian, and see how many of them can even be recalled seventy-five years after they die. This is no immortality! We remember the world's great, but you and I are not among the world's great and will not be long remembered—what about us? No, this is no immortality. This is a human fiction and mere counterfeit of it.

"Resurrection of the Dead"

Christianity believes in the on-going-ness of life after death. It does not believe, as many faiths and philosophies have believed, merely in the "immortality of the soul"—nor does it believe that our lives go back and are merged into some universal life, like a drop of water falling into the sea. We have an article written in the Creed, which says we believe in "the resurrection of the body." That does not, cannot, must not mean that all the particles of flesh that compose our human bodies—which particles we are told change completely every seven years even when we are alive—particles which have been parts of the earth or of animals or of other human beings hundreds of times over—shall all come together again in a body like that which we now wear. This must mean rather that some spiritual yet actual counterpart of the body goes on and survives, in a real and recognizable personality. It means that we shall be our selves, not some vague shadow or film of them. As God honored and dignified human bodies forever by wearing one of them, so the body is itself lifted up by resurrection to become part of the final life of man in the world to come. We see something of what the Creeds are trying to say when we remember the nature of Christ's Resurrection-body. It was material enough for Him to eat and to be recognized, though He was changed enough so that it was not easy to recognize Him always. He came, and went, even through closed doors. Was it a physical or a spiritual body? All we can say is, it was both.

What Will It Be Like?

What can be the nature of eternal life? The words are often used in the New Testament, as if the users or hearers would understand what was meant.

Sometimes it looks as if eternal life were the sum of all

the good things that Jesus gives to His followers, in answer
to the desire for all that is good that lies in every human
heart. This seems true in the passage in John 10:27,28:
"My sheep hear my voice, and I know them, and they follow me; and I give unto them eternal life . . ." Or in the great
verse, John 3:16, "God so loved the world that He gave
His only begotten Son that whosoever believeth in Him
should not perish but have everlasting life."

Sometimes and more often it seems to be life after death
to which He or others are referring in using these words. His
promise to the disciples after the refusal of the rich young
ruler was that their needs would be taken care of in this
world, they would have some persecution, "and in the world
to come eternal life." And in John 12, verse 25: "He who
loves his life loses it, and he who hates his life in this world
will keep it for eternal life."

When we think about what life will be like on the other
side, we are left with very little teaching from our Lord. The
fact of it is very clear: the nature of it is left in very dim outline. Fanciful images of golden streets are attempts to be-
speak its beauty but are not to be taken as literal descrip-
tions. Some of the spiritualists bring us very specific pictures: even cigars and armchairs seemed to figure in Sir
Oliver Lodge's picture of it. I content myself with what I
think the better wisdom of Dr. Reinhold Niebuhr when he
says, "It is unwise for Christians to claim any knowledge of
either the furniture of heaven or the temperature of hell."

Heaven As Relationships

But I think there are some things we can infer about the
nature of heaven. The most important is that we shall there
be in a condition progressing through all eternity nearer
and nearer the wonderful vision of God Himself, knowing
Him in all the sublimity of His glorious nature.

The second is like unto it. The best we know here below is relationships. There would be no life without other people, no joy nor meaning to life without their love and friendship and our relationship with them. Must not this be true in heaven also? There are some people whom I very much want to know and talk to. John Wesley is one of them. St. Francis is another. Dean Hodges (once the rector of this parish) said that it would be good to sit down in eternity and talk with St. Francis and feel you were not taking his time! But maybe there are tens of thousands and millions of others of whom we have never heard here, but who are going to be accessible to us there, and whom to know will be great joy.

Sometimes I think the best picture of heaven I ever envisioned was in a remark of G. K. Chesterton. He said it had always been his ambition to give a great party "where everybody would meet everybody else and like them very much." If heaven were nothing but a kind of continuous church service forever and ever, and angels playing on harps that Milton said never even need to be tuned, I think it would be unutterably dull. But a place where "everybody would meet everybody else and like them very much" seems to me a very reasonable and a very appealing understanding of "the communion of saints," as applies in the world to come.

I do not know what counterpart to work we shall have in heaven, but I hope there will be something, for an eternity of idleness, even if we see and know lots of interesting people, would seem without too much meaning. If there is still "growth" and progress there, maybe there is work there, too. A heaven filled with closer and closer relationships with God and people would hook on somewhat to what we already have here, and would make sense and seem desirable. But with these rather speculative thoughts about it, we must leave it, for we have few words from our Lord about its nature. We can content ourselves with remembering the phrases in the Prayer Book Collect, "such good things as pass man's understanding" and "thy promises, which exceed all that we can desire."

Faith, Not Death, Begins Eternal Life

But now I come to what I most want to say about eternal life, and that is to draw your attention to one of the most wonderful things our Lord ever said about it. It is in the 17th chapter of John, verse 3: "And this is eternal life, that they should know thee the only true God, and Jesus Christ whom thou hast sent." These are Jesus' own words, His definition of eternal life. He is praying to His Father. It is not understood in terms of duration, but of relationship. To know God and Jesus Christ is eternal life. This begins, mark you, not with death, but with faith. This does not turn our thoughts to something that is to be hereafter, but something that is to be here and now. For the knowledge of God and of His Son begins as soon as we begin to believe in God the Father and God the Son.

Here, I believe, is a doorway to faith in immortality for many people. We do not start with metaphysical speculations or doctrines, we begin with the simple approaches of discipleship. We do not begin with what happens after we are dead, we begin with a faith that can and must start on this side. How does one "know" God? Not surely by understanding all about Him, else none of us could ever begin. We know God as we begin living up to every bit of light we have, committing ourselves to Him in as full a surrender of ourselves as we can make. We know Him in the Scriptures which testify and teach about Him. We know Him when we come to know "Jesus Christ whom He hath sent." We do well to study books and learn about God and Christ. We do best when we study the Bible itself and especially as we begin to walk by faith and obey as much as we see.

Notice some other verses which confirm this thought that eternal life begins here and now. "He that believeth on the Son hath eternal life" (John 3:36), and "whoso eateth my flesh; and drinketh my blood, hath eternal life; and I will raise him up at the last day," (John 6:54), and "I write this to you who believe in the name of the Son of God, that you may know that you have eternal life."

How To Come By It

How, then, do we receive this priceless blessing of eternal life here and now and forever? When the rich young ruler asks Jesus, "What must I do to inherit eternal life?" Jesus reminded him of the Commandments, and told him his riches were standing between him and eternal life. This shows very clearly that the kind of life we live helps to determine which way we go in the life to come. We are sometimes sentimental about death, and behave as if it did not matter much what kind of life a person has lived, the funeral is just as full of hope for someone who has ignored God and done as he pleased as it is for one who has lived a saintly and unselfish life. God can work miracles, and we never know how much may have happened even in the last few moments of conscious life. But it is obviously sinful to wait so long and to leave so much to chance; we may not be conscious at the last. Let us never forget the wisdom of words like, "Be not deceived, God is not mocked; for whatsoever a man soweth that shall he also reap." Most of us ought to think more than we do about what will happen when all this world, with its friends and securities and false props is removed, and we come utterly naked as we really are into the Presence of the All-Holy. St. Paul says plainly, "The wages of sin is death." Let us ponder that plenty.

"But," he also says, "the free gift of God is eternal life in Christ Jesus" (Romans 6:23). Eternal life is a gift. It is a gift that can only be given, like all gifts, to someone who has his hands open to receive it—it will not be thrust upon us. But if we seek it by seeking God, Christ, His will for our lives, the faith by which He wants us to live, and the obedience which seals and confirms our faith, then the result is the upbuilding within us of a new and indestructible life. There is a victoriousness which you see in deeply believing people that death cannot destroy. There is a joy in them that can no more be touched by death than it is touched by the fact that life itself has hard spots in it. There is a faith in them that not only overcomes the world but overcomes death as well, that natural death which is simply a part of life for it comes to all men. There is a quality in them that is precious as no other thing in this world is precious, that has worth as no other thing in this world has worth, and which we literally cannot think of God as finally destroying—as if some great artist should fashion a beautiful painting or sculpture or vase, only to burn the painting to ashes, or dash the statue or vase to pieces on the rocks. It does not make sense to us. We cannot believe it of God. God and Christian immortality seem correlative. If you believe in God, you can't help believing in eternal life; and if you are to believe in eternal life, you must believe in God. Eternal life is His gift here and now to those who believe in Him, His indestructible gift which is never taken away. The eternity which is in Himself He imparts to us by gift. We must try to live as those to whom this gift is given, with eternity shining through us even in the midst of time. And then will come the day "when faith is lost in sight," and what now we believe, we then shall know.

God help us to believe in eternal life. God give it to us, and God help us to live as those to whom it has already been given! "And this is eternal life, that they should know thee the only true God, and Jesus Christ whom thou hast sent."

"There are those who quietly say, as their faith follows their love into the unseen, 'I know that land. Some of my people live there. Some have gone abroad on secret foreign service, which does not admit communications. But I meet from time to time the Commanding Officer, and when I mention them to Him, He assures me that all is well.'"

Dr. P. T. Forsyth

(From letter to Mrs. C.C.O. from B.J.)

Guilford, Conn.
January, 1959

Dear Mrs. O:

Since J.'s death, this family has experienced Christian friendship beyond recounting. A tremendous volume of love and concern has been lavished on all of us during the past year, and when death came to J. we were helped especially by Sam to accept the separation not as a bitter defeat, the end of everything, but as an incident in continuing life for J.

Before our experience with Sam just before the actual funeral service started becomes dimmed, I want to share it with you.

As you know, Sam came and I suggested to him that we go over the service before we went to the church so that the children would be able to follow it in the Prayer Book, and also that they might have a sort of shield against the emotion generated by the experience of strangeness I feared might permeate the Church.

I need not have worried. Our discussion with Sam went so far beyond what any of us expected that it dispelled our grief and lifted us all up. Of course, this was entirely due to Sam, for none of us could have reacted as we did without that time of prayer before we left to go to the church.

I don't have to tell you about Sam's clear, shining call by

God, his absolute faith that all catch from him. Sam was so
sure that J. was not dead, that even the kids caught this assurance about their mother, and this changed the day to one
of triumph and saw them through.

I am sure that Sam would not admit it, but I want everyone to know that it was because of Sam that we were able
to do what we did.

With love to all of you,
B. J.

(From letter to the late Rev. Canon Samuel Shoemaker from
B.Y.)

California
February 2, 1960

Dear Sam:

I have been delighted to have your very thoughtful letters.
I know your busy schedule, and it is truly wonderful that
you have found time to write so often.

I am writing now because I want to tell you of a most
wonderful experience I had last summer.

It happened last July. I had come to the clinic for another
diagnosis, and after all the tests were made and reported on,
the Doctor called me to his office. He informed me that I
had bone cancer in many parts of my body, and I did not
need to be told what that meant.

I went back to my hospital room. It was starkly drab, and
empty. It was late afternoon, and at the moment there were
no nurses or visitors on the floor. No paging of doctors, no
voices, M. had gone back home, and I was not ready to tell
her the bad news, so I was more alone than I ever had felt
before in my life. Just me and this fact about myself.

I stretched out on the bed, and I do not know how long
it was or just how to tell you about what happened. Suddenly
I felt the Presence of God flooding me with peace and a

certain kind of joy. As I remember it now, I was conscious of light, very strongly, and the light was at the right side of my bed from my head to my feet. But most real was this feeling of strength and security that poured through me. And with all this, I felt less alone than I ever felt at any time in my life. To describe it accurately is impossible. One would just have to experience it as I did to believe it.

I am sorry that my writing is too shaky for me to write this myself, but my energy is depleted. I just wanted to be sure that I told you about this without further delay.

Thank you, Sam, for all you mean, and have done for me.

B.

Author's note: B.Y. died just two weeks after dictating this letter.

EASTER EVEN

I stood, and called and called . . .
But there was no answer.
My little surroundings lengthened out into the universe itself.
I was calling within it,
And it became like a vast, empty corridor—
An empty corridor with great rounded shoulder-arches
That seemed to enclose infinite space.
But it was all empty and cold—
With that emptiness that has been empty for years,
For centuries, for aeons . . .
It was a space that called to be filled.
An emptiness that was cavernous with vacancy.
I called and called . . .
But there was no answer, save the echo of my own voice
Coming back to mock itself.
It was like the reflectors by the side of the road,
Which have no light in themselves, but only send back

The light of our own headlights.
It was vast and cold and empty.

And I waited. I had to wait.
I had to wait until Easter Even . . .
And then suddenly Voices began to come.
They burst out that morning in a chorus . . .
They couldn't hold back till Easter day, they unleashed
    themselves
Like unmanageable steeds, they poured out like cataracts of
    great water.
The stars called out, and the planets, and the sun and moon,
And all the inter-stellar space caught up in their sound in a
    mighty echo,
Till the whole universe was sounding with Voices . . .
All of them said the same thing, said it in deafening chorus,
Said it coming at me in such mass and quantity,
Said it so many ways and so insistently,
Said it so that my heart heard it unmistakeably,
And I knew it was the universe's delayed answer to me.

And the burden of the song of the spheres
Was caught up by the mountains and the seas
And it flowed with the rivers, and it spoke out of the skies.
It kept leaping out from the inwardness of things,
And pointed itself at me like a million million
Little spiritual rapiers, pointed right at me
Who had called into the empty corridors.
And the song they all sang
Was a hymn I had loved since my childhood,
Loved more than I ever loved any hymn . . .
And it went
"Jesus Christ is risen today . . . alleluia."

Samuel Moor Shoemaker

CREDO

August, 1963

As I sit in the study on a beautiful, cool August afternoon, I look back with many thanks. It has been a great run. I wouldn't have missed it for anything. Much could and should have been better, and I have, by no means, done what I should have done with all that I have been given. But the overall experience of being alive has been a thrilling experience. I believe that death is a doorway to more of it—clearer, cleaner, better, with more of the secret opened than unlocked. I do not feel much confidence in myself as regards all this, for very few have ever "deserved" eternal life. But with Christ's atonement and Him gone on before, I have neither doubt nor fear whether I am left here a brief time or a long one. I believe that I shall see Him and know Him, and that eternity will be an endless opportunity to consort with the great souls and the lesser ones who have entered into the freedom of the heavenly city. It is His forgiveness and grace that gives confidence and not merits of our own. But again I say, it's been a great run. I'm thankful for it and for all the people who have helped make it so, and especially those closest and dearest to me.

Samuel Moor Shoemaker

(Excerpt from letter from Mr. B. W., Co-founder of A.A., to C.C.O.)

New York, New York
February 25, 1964

Dear Mrs. O:

It was good to know that you, too, had the privilege of being at Sam's funeral. Never had I thought to witness such a demonstration of faith, and even of confident joy.

Sincerely,
B. W.

(Excerpts from talk given by P.M.O., Jr. at a Memorial
Service for S.M.S. at Calvary Church, New York on November 10, 1963.)

"Since last week when Sam left us, many memories come
crowding, memories of his and my fellowship on trips we
took together, and of the response Sam always got from the
men and women in his audiences.

"There was a wonderful release in Sam for the tensions in
our lives. Much of the stress and strain vanished from men's
faces when Sam talked about his faith. Healthy laughter
came from them as he spoke. By the time Sam was finished
men seemed strangely incorporated into a warm and loving
fellowship.

"A strong sun—a man of great conviction about God and
Jesus Christ—was burning away the mists. The Holy Spirit
was doing what He always did when He came through Sam,
that is bringing people into unity as their hearts were released by God.

"In closing, Sam will continue to be a powerful inspiration,
the same inspiration he has been all the years he was with
us. But no—he is with us now. I can see his smile; I can hear
his chuckle. Long ago Sam gave me some words of leave-
taking from this world written by an Indian philosopher.
They go like this:

"'I am standing on the seashore. A ship at my side spreads
her white sails to the morning breeze and starts for the blue
ocean. She is an object of beauty and strength, and I stand
and watch her until, at length, she hangs like a speck of
white cloud just where the sky and sea mingle with each
other.

"'Then someone at my side says, "There! She is gone!" Gone
where? Gone from my sight, that is all. She is just as large in

mast and hull and spar as she was when she left my side, and she is just as able to bear her load of living freight to her destination. Her diminished size is in me, not in her!

" 'And just at that moment when someone at my side says, "There! She is gone!" there are other eyes watching her coming, and other voices ready to take up the glad shout, "There she comes!" ' " And this, I'm sure, has been Sam's welcome."

APPENDIX

APPENDIX

The many national and international movements for Christ's Kingdom, either initiated by Sam Shoemaker or nurtured by him, or both, are a living monument to his memory.

Letters from leaders in these movements about "Dr. Sam" are given here because they are a reflection of the character of the man himself.

(From letter to Mrs. C.C.O. from Mr. Jim Rayburn, Executive Director of Young Life Campaign, one of the movements for youth sponsored by Dr. Shoemaker.)

Colorado Springs
Colorado
April 4, 1964

Dear Mrs. O:

Thank you for your letter of April 3 concerning the collection of Sam's sermons. I am glad to hear that this is being done.

I was indeed saddened at Sam's death and miss him very much.

To me, Sam Shoemaker excelled in following the example of our Lord in his attitude toward people, and truly he was the "friend of publicans and sinners."

Beyond that he loved any and all work that pointed men to Christ.

I do not know of a leader in our generation who surpassed

him in his marvelous capacity to open-heartedly back every effort, no matter how small or "independent," to make Christ known to our troubled world. For this and many other reasons he blessed my life as few men ever have done, and the lives of all the people of the Young Life Staff with whom he came in contact.

We thank God for him. We miss him greatly.

Thank you for including us.

Cordially,

J. R.

(From letter to Mrs. C. C. O. from Dr. John L. Peters, President of "World Neighbors")

Oklahoma City, Oklahoma
March 6, 1964

Dear Mrs. O:

I am just home from India and Africa on a World Neighbors mission, and your letter has just been read. I count it a privilege to try to pay tribute to our beloved Sam.

Sam Shoemaker was one of the "Founding Fathers" of World Neighbors, and of many other movements for God and for man.

As "new wine" bursts old bottles, the spirit of Sam bursts through every poor attempt to pay him tribute. Old ways never contained him, and old words cannot portray him. Sam gave to World Neighbors his solicitous guidance, unqualified support; his guidance shaped its course and spurred its growth.

World Neighbors is only one of many creative movements which will live on; a selfless monument to Sam's matchless spirit.

We will watch with interest the progress of the book, and rejoice that it will be ours to read.

Sincerely,

J. P.

(From letter from the Rev. Donald T. James, Executive Director of the Pittsburgh Experiment, to Mrs. C.C.O.)

Pittsburgh, Pa.
June 4, 1964

Dear Mrs. O:

If I were to pick one word that best explained Dr. Sam's influence on the lives of those of us in The Pittsburgh Experiment, that one word would be LOVE.

Because of his great love of God and man, Dr. Sam first attracted us, then shared with us his logical reasons for seeking and finding the Father, the Son, and the Holy Spirit, who makes real love possible.

In The Pittsburgh Experiment, Dr. Sam brought together into small groups the privileged, the average, and the underprivileged. He helped us to realize that God loved each of us, and that, in turn, we had a responsibility to be concerned for, to share with, and to love each other.

He directed us to get changed, to get together, and to get going! And he told us how to do it; to get changed we were to commit our lives to Christ, and through prayer and seeking in church and elsewhere, to learn and to do God's will.

To get together, to share our experiments and experiences as we tried to be new people in Christ, there are many prayer groups meeting still; and Dr. Sam insisted that we get going out into the world, as far as we could reach, to spread the Good News, as ambassadors.

These were Dr. Sam's ideas for The Pittsburgh Experiment, and we who are carrying on for Dr. Sam are doing these things on a growing scale.

Sincerely,
D. T. J.

(From letter to Mrs. C.C.O. from Mr. Kirk B. Cunningham, Chairman of Board of The Pittsburgh Experiment.)

Dear Mrs. O:

Thank you for telling me of the book you are doing about our friend, Dr. Sam. He was a great man, one who really cared about people.

His vision for Pittsburgh, as he tried to implement it, was that Pittsburgh become a city on fire for God, as famous for God as it is for steel.

From that first group of laymen he challenged to experiment with the idea of Christ as a daily partner in work situations, prayer and discussion groups at the job level have sprung up throughout the city. Dr. Sam pointed his finger at one man after another with the searching question, "What are you doing about all this?"

His Experiment has changed many lives and made its influence felt at all levels in the very heart of Pittsburgh.

I am proud and glad to have known this man, and to be a part of The Pittsburgh Experiment he started.

Love,
K. B. C.

(Letter from Dr. Elton Trueblood, Author and Lecturer, to Mrs. C.C.O.)

Earlham College
Richmond, Indiana
May 11, 1964

Dear Mrs. O:

As one eager to honor the late Sam Shoemaker, I am glad to express my love and admiration for him.

I can say it very simply. In a day of great confusion, Sam Shoemaker was clear. He proved that it is possible to be both an intellectual and an evangelistic.

Sincerely,
E. T.

(From letter to Mrs. C.C.O. from Emily Gardiner Neal,

author of "A Reporter Finds God Through Spiritual Healing," "God Can Heal You Now," "In the Midst of Life," etc.)

Dear C:

All blessings on the book about Sam. I can only say that to me he was one of the Episcopal Church's greatest; an evangelist in the truest sense of the word. Sam really cannot be claimed by one branch of the Christian Church alone. His influence extended far beyond the confines of denominationalism. He was known to, and beloved by, Christians everywhere! His converts are to be found in every nook and cranny of the United States, and far beyond. "Dr. Sam" belongs to the Church Universal.

"The most tremendous thing in the world," he once said, "is for men to find the door to God." To this door he has led thousands of seeking souls; upon its latch he has placed thousands of groping hands.

His physical voice may be silenced now, but through the written word his genius in meeting people where they are, his warmth, his love, his wit, his passion to bring men to Christ still eloquently speak.

Lovingly,
E. N.

(From letter to Mrs. C.C.O. from the late Mr. Branch Rickey, Manager, Pittsburgh Pirates and St. Louis Cardinals)

Dear Mrs. O:

I did not meet Dr. Shoemaker while in Pittsburgh as somehow our paths never crossed. But, although I had admired him and wanted to meet him, it did not come about until we were both at a convention of the movement called Christian Athletes in the West shortly after that movement got underway.

After that, and because of this mutual interest, Canon Shoemaker and I came to know each other well, and I remember a broadcast he gave about Christian Athletes in which he gave it his warm approval.

To me, Canon Shoemaker was truly Christian, a minister who gave meaning not only to life, but to immortality.

And not only was he deeply devoted, but he was intelligent and informed. He meant much to me and to thousands of others in our movement, Christian Athletes.

> Cordially,
> B. R.

(From letter to Mrs. C.C.O. from the Reverend Tom Parker, Methodist Minister in South Africa.)

> Durban, South Africa
> December 9, 1963

Dear Mrs. O:

I was so very sorry to learn from your letter that Dr. Shoemaker had died.

He was a great man. I consider him the modern John Wesley of the Christian Church.

He will be greatly missed by many of us out here as many received T.W.W., and his sermons were the greatest help I had in my own ministry outside of the Bible itself.

Kindest regards, and I will watch for the book.

> Sincerely,
> T. P.

(From letter to Mrs. C.C.O. from the Honorable Walter H. Judd)

> Washington, D. C.
> August 6, 1964

Dear Mrs. O:

I am sorry to have been so long in answering your letter

about the book of sermons of Sam Shoemaker's which you are planning.

My respect and affection for Dr. Sam were so great that I want to include my word, for the benefit of my own soul, although what I can say of him does seem to me superfluous.

For me, Dr. Sam had no superior—as a preacher, a pastor, a prophet, a pioneer. And he had that extraordinary ability to separate the important from the trivial, to see need in people who had it, right through whatever external shell existed. Gently, and in love, he would probe and appeal to the deepest in all whose lives he touched.

His ministry was as wholesome and healing to the missionary as to the alcoholic. His words live after him, and his life ministers to us and always will.

> Very sincerely yours,
> W. H. J.

(From letter to Mrs. C.C.O. from Mrs. H.J.)

> Evanston, Ill.
> December 15. 1963

Dear Mrs. O:

Yes, we had heard that our beloved Dr. Shoemaker died on All Saints' Day. How appropriate, although he was the most *human* saint anyone ever knew. That was why so many loved him, that plus his great capacity for love.

In one of his writings, Dr. Norman Vincent Peale has said, "If I were asked to name five of the greatest preachers in the United States today, Sam Shoemaker would be right at the top of the list." Then Dr. Peale went on to say that he had been talking with a young man from Pittsburgh who had mentioned Dr. Sam with great affection, and when asked why he loved Sam so much, the young man answered, 'Because Sam helped me to find a self I never knew I had.'

I used to have a friend who said that Sam Shoemaker

loved people into the Kingdom of Heaven. Indeed, he was a great artist at loving people.

We will miss him, and his writings, so it is fine that you are collecting a few for a book from T.W.W. Be sure and let me know how you come along.

Cordially,
H. J.

(From letter to Mrs. C.C.O. from Dr. Abraham Vereide, Founder of International Christian Leadership.)

Washington, D. C.
May 22, 1964

Dear Mrs. O:

Thank you for your letter of May 8th.

Sam Shoemaker was one of the most constructive, understanding, and helping friends a man or woman could have. This was, among other things, because he was unsparingly honest and surgically helpful, though he always told the truth with love.

Sam was God's man, and he made a lasting contribution to Christendom as a whole, and, since he was an Episcopalian, his influence was especially felt in the Episcopal and the Anglican Church.

I am grateful for the opportunity to express my feeling for Sam and wish you Godspeed with this effort to project his ministry into the future.

Sincerely,
A. V.

Excerpts from Bishop's Memorial:

DR. SAMUEL M. SHOEMAKER,
LEADING EVANGELIST
BY
THE RIGHT REVEREND BISHOP AUSTIN PARDUE,
BISHOP OF PITTSBURGH

On the eve of All Saints' Day, 1963, "Sam" Shoemaker passed to Paradise. Dr. Shoemaker was unquestionably one of the greatest evangelists this Church has ever produced. I am sure that most of us would agree with this evaluation made by *Living Church*, one of our national Episcopal magazines.

Dr. Shoemaker was dominated by a passion for the conversion of souls. He was something like John Wesley in that there was no man he feared to challenge on behalf of his Lord and Saviour.

Sam had an almost incorrigible sense of humor. I have never laughed more heartily with anyone than with this great man. He had a built-in kind of electricity which fairly crackled with vigor, energy and magnetism.

Among other movements, Sam was one of the founders of AA, and he knew men in their depths of despair, and has helped an almost unlimited number of men and women who had alcoholic problems. There are many virtues I could mention, but it would be unfair to Dr. Shoemaker to make him out a saint for he would be the first to be embarrassed by an unofficial canonization. It is enough to say that Sam was one of the greatest Christian personalities I ever knew, probably the most unique and the most effective. As his Bishop and personal pastor, I shall never cease to thank God for Sam's innumerable gifts to the needs of the souls of men.

(From a memorial sermon for Canon Shoemaker preached on November 11, 1963 at Calvary Episcopal Church, Pittsburgh, Pa., by its rector, The Rev. Dr. John Baiz.)

"What a great soldier for Christ was our late Rector, Sam Shoemaker! Recently, someone said to me, 'Sam was born with a Baptist heart into an Episcopal family.'

"As Sam's Bishop, Bishop Pardue, put it, 'Sam was totally in love with Christ and he tried to get everyone to share that love with him. He presented Christ to personal lives and to social structures and was caught up in a magnificent zest for God and for life.' "

(From letter to Mrs. C.C.O. from Dr. Sherwood S. Day)
Co-founder of "Faith at Work" Movement.

Amerst, Virginia
May 13, 1964

Dear Mrs. O:

I am indeed grateful to be able to write something of the way I feel about Sam Shoemaker. There are two thoughts that I should like to focus upon in talking of my friend, and they are: Sam was willing and ready to become involved in every work of the Spirit no matter under what flag, and, of course, I know best of his involvement with *Faith at Work* Magazine because we worked together on this when the magazine was called the *Evangel* and went out from Calvary Church in New York. The magazine *Evangel* was especially close to Sam's heart, and now that it has become a movement, dedicated to introducing men and women all over the world to Jesus Christ, the movement more than ever reflects Sam's ecumenical spirit.

Such men live on in their works. I ·shall look forward to his book.

Sincerely,
S. S. D.

Quoted by permission from *Grapevine*, January, 1964, magazine published by Alcoholics Anonymous.

IN MEMORY OF DR. SAM
By B. W.

On Thursday, October 31, 1963, Dr. Sam Shoemaker, the great Episcopal clergyman and first friend of A. A., passed from our sight and hearing. He was one of those few without whose ministration A. A. could never have been born in the first place nor prospered since.

From his teaching Dr. Bob and I absorbed most of the principles that were later embodied in the Twelve Steps of A. A. Our ideas of self-examination, acknowledgement of character defects, restitution for harms done, and working with others came straight from Sam. Therefore, he gave to us the concrete knowledge of what we could do about our illness; he passed to us the spiritual keys by which so many of us have since been liberated.

We who in A. A.'s early time were privileged to fall under the spell of his inspiration can never be the same again.

We shall bless Sam's memory forever.

STATEMENT BY MAYOR JOSEPH M. BARR
CITY OF PITTSBURGH, PENNSYLVANIA
THURSDAY, NOVEMBER 7, 1963

The City of Pittsburgh has experienced a keen sense of loss with the death of Dr. Samuel Shoemaker. As pastor of Calvary Episcopal Church of Pittsburgh from 1952 through 1961, as Canon of the Episcopal Diocese of Pittsburgh, and as a well-known counselor of the business community, Dr. Shoemaker was instrumental in beginning a spiritual renaissance of the city, to undergird its material renaissance.

Many citizens of Pittsburgh will remember well his weekly

Sunday night radio program, "Faith That Works," in which he brought counsel and comfort to the problems of the city with his bright and clear interpretation of faith.

Pittsburghers were gratified, but not surprised, when Dr. Shoemaker in 1955 was named one of the ten greatest preachers in the United States by a national magazine.

The message which Dr. Sam brought to Pittsburgh during his decade in Pittsburgh was never a bland or a quiet one. He attacked all of the backward failings of humanity with fierceness, wit and relevancy. But Dr. Sam was never pessimistic. He saw, and made others. see, a shining future for Pittsburgh as a city under God.

(From letter to Mrs. C.C.O. from Mr. Ralston Young, widely known as "Red-cap Forty-two" of Grand Central Station, N.Y.)

Dear Mrs. O:

Dr. Sam was my friend, and I remember him as one of God's Apostles.

So deeply did he love the Lord and his fellow man that God's love seemed to flow through him to all he met.

Sincerely,
R. Y.